DISCARD

ABC OF CONFLICT AND DISASTER

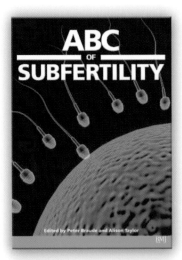
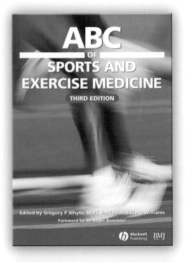
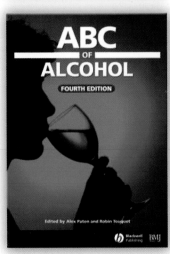
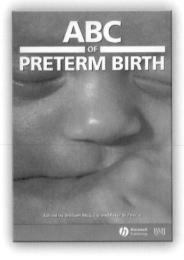

ABC OF CONFLICT AND DISASTER

Edited by

ANTHONY D REDMOND
Emeritus professor of emergency medicine, Keele University, North Staffordshire

PETER F MAHONEY
Senior lecturer, Academic Department of Military Emergency Medicine,
Royal Centre for Defence Medicine, Birmingham

JAMES M RYAN
Leonard Cheshire professor of conflict recovery, University College London, London
and international professor of surgery, Uniformed Services University of the Health Sciences (USUHS), Bethesda, MD, USA

and

CARA MACNAB
Research fellow, Leonard Cheshire Centre of Conflict Recovery,
University College London, London

BMJ
Books

Blackwell
Publishing

© 2006 by Blackwell Publishing Ltd
BMJ Books is an imprint of the BMJ Publishing Group Limited, used under licence

Blackwell Publishing Inc., 350 Main Street, Malden, Massachusetts 02148-5020, USA
Blackwell Publishing Ltd, 9600 Garsington Road, Oxford OX4 2DQ, UK
Blackwell Publishing Asia Pty Ltd, 550 Swanston Street, Carlton, Victoria 3053, Australia

First published 2006

Library of Congress Cataloging-in-Publication Data
ABC of conflict and disaster/edited by Anthony D. Redmond ... [et al.].
       p. ; cm.
   Includes bibliographical references and index.
   ISBN-13: 978-0-7279-1726-3
   ISBN-10: 0-7279-1726-9
   1. Disasters—Health aspects. 2. Health risk assessment. 3. Disaster relief. I. Redmond, Anthony D.
   [DNLM: 1. Disasters. 2. Emergency Medical Services. WA 295 A134 2006]

   RA645.5.A22 2006
   363.34′8—dc22

                                                                                        2005022942

ISBN-13: 978 0 7279 1726 3
ISBN-10: 0 7279 1726 9

A catalogue record for this title is available from the British Library

Cover image is courtesy of Bernard Bisson/CORBIS SYGMA

Set by BMJ Electronic Production
Printed and bound in Spain by GraphyCems, Navarra

Commissioning Editor: Eleanor Lines
Editorial Assistant: Ariel Vernon
Development Editors: Sally Carter/Nick Morgan
Senior Technical Editor: Greg Cotton
Production Controller: Debbie Wyer

For further information on Blackwell Publishing, visit our website:
http://www.blackwellpublishing.com

The publisher's policy is to use permanent paper from mills that operate a sustainable forestry policy, and which
has been manufactured from pulp processed using acid-free and elementary chlorine-free practices. Furthermore,
the publisher ensures that the text paper and cover board used have met acceptable environmental accreditation
standards.

29.95   1/4/07

Contents

Contributors

Ewan W Anderson
Emeritus professor of geopolitics, University of Durham, Durham

Marion Birch
Training manager, International Health Exchange/RedR, London

Martin C M Bricknell
Chief medical adviser, Headquarters Allied Rapid Reaction Corps, Germany

Eddie Chaloner
Consultant vascular surgeon, University Hospital Lewisham, London

Derek Gardener
Biomedical laboratory scientific officer, University of Liverpool, Department of Pathology, Royal Liverpool University Hospital, Liverpool

Christine Gosden
Professor of medical genetics, University of Liverpool, Department of Pathology, Royal Liverpool University Hospital, Liverpool

Maria Kett
Research fellow, Leonard Cheshire Centre of Conflict Recovery, University College London, London

Tracey MacCormack
Health service attraction and retention officer, Canadian Forces Health Services Group Headquarters, Ottawa, Ontario, Canada

Cara Macnab
Research fellow, Leonard Cheshire Centre of Conflict Recovery, University College London, London

Sarah Maguire
Independent international human rights consultant, London

Peter F Mahoney
Senior lecturer, Academic Department of Military Emergency Medicine, Royal Centre for Defence Medicine, Birmingham

Steve J Mannion
Consultant orthopaedic surgeon and honorary lecturer, Leonard Cheshire Centre of Conflict Recovery, University College London, London

Simon Miller
Parkes professor of preventive medicine, Army Medical Directorate, FASC, Camberley

Eric K Noji
Senior medical officer, Centers for Disease Control and Prevention, Washington Office, USA

Ian Palmer
Professor of military psychiatry, Division of Psychological Medicine, Institute of Psychiatry, London

Jonathan Potter
Executive Director, People In Aid, London

The Project Manager
Sphere Project, Geneva, Switzerland

Anthony D Redmond
Emeritus professor of emergency medicine, Keele University, North Staffordshire

James M Ryan
Leonard Cheshire Professor of conflict recovery, University College London and international professor of surgery, Uniformed Services University of the Health Sciences (UHUHS), Bethesda, MD, USA

John Seaman
Independent consultant in overseas development, Kent

World Health Organization
Department for Health Action in Crises, WHO, Geneva, Switzerland

Foreword

This *ABC of Conflict and Disaster* is both an excellent idea and is extremely well executed. It deserves to become a constant companion not just of doctors but also nurses and health workers and people from the many other disciplines which contribute to humanitarian relief work. When active in the field facing a myriad of problems, there is a need for an easily accessible and reliable guide to action and prevention. This book provides all this with much cumulated wisdom.

One of the most attractive aspects of humanitarian assistance is how much genuine cooperation is now developing between the UN agencies, the Red Cross and the Red Crescent, NGOs, specialized government departments and organizations as diverse as Médecins Sans Frontières, RedR and International Health Exchange, along with many others too numerous to list. I am of course proud of what the UK has contributed and is continuing to contribute in this field. But we all know that our effort is part of a multinational response. We are all on a learning curve, adapting, adjusting and reinforcing our knowledge from the all important vantage point of actual experience on the ground, grappling with everyday realities.

My own involvement in this area goes back to the very nearly three years which I spent on behalf of the EU negotiating in tandem with the UN in the former Yugoslavia from 1992 to 1995. I saw then how many people thirsted for more knowledge to help them in their multiple humanitarian tasks. They faced at times an overwhelming challenge of trying to deliver aid while a war continued, endless ceasefires were broken and peace eluded us all, mainly because the permanent members of the Security Council were not ready to enforce a settlement. I vowed then to try to do all I could to help bridge that gap.

I hope this book will enrich your experience and become a trusted friend.

Lord David Owen

1 Humanitarian assistance: standards, skills, training, and experience

Marion Birch, Simon Miller

Standards for humanitarian agencies

The Sphere Project

Those affected by catastrophe and conflicts often lose basic human rights. Recognising this, a group of humanitarian non-governmental organisations and the Red Cross movement launched the Sphere Project in 1997. The aim of this project was to improve the quality of assistance and enhance the accountability of the humanitarian system in disaster response by developing a set of universal minimum standards in core areas and a humanitarian charter.

The charter, based on international treaties and conventions, emphasises the right of people affected by disaster to life with dignity. It identifies the protection of this right as a quality measure of humanitarian work and one for which humanitarian actors bear responsibilities.

The Sphere Project was launched in response to concern about inconsistencies in aid provided to people affected by disaster, and the frequent lack of accountability of humanitarian agencies to their beneficiaries, their membership, and their donors. The project attempts to identify and define the rights of populations affected by disasters in order to facilitate effective planning and implementation of humanitarian relief.

People in Aid: human resources management

People in Aid was founded with two main aims—to highlight the importance of human resources management in the effective achievement of an organisation's mission, and to offer support to humanitarian and development agencies wishing to improve human resources management.

After the Rwanda crisis, research showed that aid workers saw organisational and management issues as prime stressors in their work. From this research, the People in Aid *Code of Good Practice* was developed. The code focuses on the organisational decisions that affect aid workers—such as including human resources in plans and budgets, risk management, and communicating with staff on human resources issues. It helps agencies to assess their own human resources policies, practice, training, and monitoring. People in Aid awards "kite marks" (using the social auditing process) to those agencies that implement the code.

Gaining skills and experience

Training

Complex emergencies typically involve large numbers of refugees or internally displaced people, conflict or threat of conflict, a high risk of epidemics, and disruption of normal infrastructure. UK training as a nurse or a doctor is unlikely to prepare health workers adequately for such conditions. While each crisis scenario has unique problems, there are common themes that, if addressed through training, can prepare people to work effectively in any emergency situation.

Public health in emergencies course—Run by the International Health Exchange and Merlin, it uses trainers with field experience to give overviews of public health interventions. It includes sessions on communicable diseases, health centre management, nutrition, reproductive and mental health, and HIV infection and AIDS.

Refugee camp in Darfur, Sudan, 1985. Refugees from the drought and conflict in Chad had been brought by truck from further up the border between Chad and Sudan before the rains came, so that they would not be cut off from outside aid during the rainy season

---

What does the Sphere Project cover?

The Sphere handbook provides minimum standards common to all key sectors of humanitarian aid
- Water supply, sanitation, and hygiene promotion
- Food security and nutrition
- Food aid
- Shelter, settlement, and non-food items
- Health services

People in Aid *Code of Good Practice*

The code covers issues vital in the management of aid workers
- Learning, training, and development
- Briefing and debriefing
- Performance management and support
- Motivation and reward

Characteristics of humanitarian crises that aid workers may need to prepare for

- Large numbers of refugees or internally displaced people in need of help
- Normal services and infrastructure severely disrupted
- Conflict or threat of conflict
- Increased risk of communicable disease outbreaks
- Communities affected by physical and mental trauma

1

Liverpool School of Tropical Medicine diploma in humanitarian assistance—This is run in partnership with Liverpool University and leading non-governmental organisations. Core modules cover the political, economic, and legal context of humanitarian assistance and consider planning and management at all stages of humanitarian crises.

Catastrophes and conflict course—Run by the Society of Apothecaries of London, this modular course covers the spectrum of humanitarian intervention. Vivas and a dissertation lead to the diploma in the medical care of catastrophes (DMCC).

Other courses cover issues that are important for all aspects of humanitarian work. ActionAid has developed a set of training modules on the rights-based approach. Oxfam, in collaboration with the International Health Exchange, has developed a course on "gender issues in humanitarian assistance."

Gaining experience

Most agencies require two years' post-qualification experience. However, gaining primary field experience can be a "Catch 22" situation, as many agencies ask for experience overseas before they will consider a candidate. Language skills, experience of living abroad, and specific skills help.

The main thing is not to lose heart. The human resources departments of agencies are very busy and may not have time to reply. Join the register of a recruiting agency (such as the International Health Exchange, RedR), send your curriculum vitae to organisations and follow up by telephone, and keep an eye on job vacancies advertised in newspapers (such as the Wednesday *Guardian*) and the websites of aid organisations.

However keen you may be to get a job, ensure you ask about any key issues not already covered in the job description. Check terms and conditions, including arrangements for health care, and ask about the organisation's security policy where appropriate. The People in Aid code of conduct lays out a framework and minimum standards for human resource management in emergencies.

Get as much information as you can about where you are going before you go. Do not limit yourself to information specifically about your job; find out about the history of the country, the present political situation, cultural and social norms, and basic health information.

Be aware that the situation is dynamic and may change by the time you arrive. Often the most important aspect of what you manage to learn before you leave is that it prepares you for the right questions to ask. Potential sources of information include the internet (including academic, government, and agency websites), journals and books, aid agencies' reports, and embassy briefings.

Maintaining skills

The ever changing political landscape, ongoing research, and new strategies mean that in-service training is important for humanitarian workers. You can keep up to date in the field by reading journals and newsletters such as the International Health Exchange's *Health Exchange* magazine and those from the Overseas Development Institute and Healthlink Worldwide. The internet has made a huge difference, but, as with all subjects, information should be cross checked if it is not from a known and credible source. Take time off to attend courses, share experiences with others, and step back and think.

Two examples of areas where practice is changing quickly are nutrition and HIV/AIDS. Therapeutic feeding schedules are far more refined than they were, and special feeding products are readily available. Exciting new initiatives in home based feeding are being piloted. HIV/AIDS is by far the biggest recent challenge in health and has important implications for

Shanty town behind the port in Luanda, the capital of Angola. People displaced by conflict in the provinces sought shelter in Luanda, and an infrastructure designed for 600 000 people struggled to cope with 3 000 000. People chose to live near the port, despite the area being subject to flooding and erosion, because it offered casual labour

Useful websites for training and information in humanitarian agencies

Aidworker	www.aidworker.com
AlertNet	www.alertnet.org/
International Health Exchange	www.ihe.org.uk
Merlin	www.merlin.org.uk
People in Aid	www.peopleinaid.org
RedR	www.redr.org
ReliefWeb	www.reliefweb.int/
Society of Apothecaries	www.apothecaries.org.uk
The Sphere Project	www.sphereproject.org
Center for International Health and Cooperation	www.cihc.org

Types of information to be considered before deploying to a crisis situation

- Historical
- Geographical
- Political
- Religious
- Cultural
- Social
- Health
- Prevailing circumstances

Therapeutic feeding centre in a camp in Darfur, Sudan, for Chadian refugees, 1985. In such centres, where the most malnourished children are treated, the children should have as much stimulation and as normal a life as possible, not only with their parents but with other children humanitarian assistance. Research into, for example, mother to child transmission and breast feeding is ongoing, and it is important to keep up with the latest developments.

Teams in the field

You will almost certainly be part of a team working closely alongside local agencies. Good coordination within your team is essential, and this should be based on a clear understanding of each other's roles and responsibilities, and how these contribute to the overall objectives. It must be clear who is responsible for security issues. Sufficient leave and breaks should be taken, as they will contribute to good relationships in the field.

The health and safety of aid workers

Some areas are more hostile for humanitarian workers than they used to be. It is important that your organisation has a good understanding of the situation and briefs you well. Road traffic crashes are responsible for many injuries and deaths among aid workers. Sometimes the hardest thing is to follow rules about who should drive and when, especially out of normal working hours, but this is crucial for health and safety. RedR runs a range of security courses, details of which can be found on its website.

Taking care of your own health is essential; your agency should advise you on immunisations and malaria prophylaxis, what drugs to take, and arrangements for care and evacuation. Just as important as malaria prophylaxis is avoiding mosquito bites with insect repellents, impregnated mosquito nets, and suitable clothing. Travel clinics, the Department of Health, and organisations such as Interhealth offer clear guidance.

Cultural awareness

Remember that life didn't start for anyone when you got off the plane. Your intervention needs to fit into the local response to the crisis. You must be aware of what has already been done and find out from local people the most acceptable way to go about things. Pre-deployment reading will help you to understand local norms and practice. Remember that people will not expect you to know everything—if in doubt ask what is appropriate for you, as an outsider, to do.

In trying to understand local culture, you may find that you cannot agree with some part of it. If this has implications for your work you need to discuss this with your manager. When deciding whether to react, it can help to ask yourself what difference it is going to make to those you are trying to assist. What will be the likely end result for them?

Funding

The amount of funding for programmes and projects, and the way it is provided, has a great influence on their scope. Your organisation may have made a proposal to get specific funding for a particular disaster, it may use funds it already has, or it may issue a joint appeal for funds through a mechanism such as the Disasters Emergency Committee in Britain.

Training is funded in various ways. Your agency may pay as part of staff development. Grants are sometimes available. Many workers fund their own training, and courses such as those run by the International Health Exchange, Merlin, and RedR are subsidised to make this less difficult.

The sections on the Sphere Project and People in Aid were supplied by the project manager, Sphere Project, Geneva, Switzerland, and Jonathan Potter, executive director, People in Aid, London.

Competing interests: None declared.

Community worker giving out chlorine for water disinfection in a shanty town in Luanda, Angola. This is one strategy for preventing cholera and is done in conjunction with intensive health promotion to ensure the correct use of chlorine

Road traffic crashes represent one of the main dangers for aid workers in the field

Disasters Emergency Committee Agencies

- Action Aid (www.actionaid.org)
- CAFOD (www.cafod.org.uk)
- Care (www.care.org)
- Concern (www.concern.ie)
- Help the Aged (www.helptheaged.org)
- Save the Children (www.savethechildren.org)
- British Red Cross (www.redcross.org.uk)
- Christian Aid (www.christian – aid.org.uk)
- Merlin (www.merlin.org.uk)
- Oxfam (www.oxfam.org.uk)
- Tearfund (www.tearfund.org)
- World Vision (www. wvi.org)

Further reading

- Medécins Sans Frontières. *Refugee health—an approach to emergency situations.* London: Macmillan, 1997
- Chin J, ed. *Control of communicable diseases manual.* 17th ed. Washington, DC: American Public Health Association, 2000
- Webber R. *Communicable disease epidemiology and control.* Wallingford: CABI Publishing, 1996
- Ryan J, Mahoney PF, Greaves I, Bowyer G, eds. *Conflict and catastrophe medicine: a practical guide.* London: Springer-Verlag, 2002
- Department of Health. *Immunisation against infectious disease.* London: HMSO, 1996
- Department of Health. *Health information for overseas travel.* London: HMSO, 1995
- Cutts M, Dingle A. Safety first: protecting NGO employees who work in areas of conflict. London: Save the Children, 1998

2   Natural disasters

Anthony D Redmond

Disasters are commonly divided into "natural" and "man made," but such distinctions are generally artificial. All disasters are fundamentally human made, a function of where and how people choose or are forced to live. The trigger may be a natural phenomenon such as an earthquake, but its impact is governed by the prior vulnerability of the affected community.

Poverty is the single most important factor in determining vulnerability: poor countries have weak infrastructure, and poor people cannot afford to move to safer places. Whatever the disaster, the main threat to health often comes from the mass movement of people away from the scene and into inadequate temporary facilities.

International medical aid

Local medical services may be disrupted and require international help, not only in dealing with the effects of the disaster but also to maintain routine health facilities for unrelated conditions. An often overlooked aspect of medical need is the rehabilitation of those disabled by the disaster. Help in this regard can be provided in a planned and measured fashion and is often required for years.

The effectiveness of international surgical teams is limited by the delay in getting to a disaster area. However, outside medical and surgical help may be needed in the post-emergency phase. International aid can help national and local authorities to restore routine medical and surgical facilities overwhelmed by the disaster and may support later specialist elective services.

Survivors with crush injury invariably stimulate requests for international aid in the use of dialysis. This is a complex issue raising difficult questions about sustainability and appropriate use of limited resources. As with much aid in complex circumstances, this is best negotiated with guidance from international aid organisations and agencies such as the International Society of Nephrologists.

Types of disaster

Earthquakes
Movements of the Earth's crust create tremors below ground every day; fortunately the vast majority are out at sea. The point nearest to the surface is the epicentre and marks the site where the quake is strongest. Force is measured on the Richter scale—a logarithmic scale, so that a force 7 quake is 10 times stronger than force 6 and 100 times stronger than force 5. When earthquakes occur near to or on land, the major danger is from building collapse. Survivability is not always related to building height. Falling debris and entrapment pose the greatest risks.

Search and rescue
Most successful rescues take place within the first 24 hours. Most lives are saved by the immediate actions of survivors. Local authorities implement the second phase, when a more coordinated response is established with local rescue teams joining the survivors. In the third phase more intensive and focused efforts are supplemented with extra help from other areas. The fourth and final phase involves the provision of specialist aid for rescuing people deeply entrapped.

Most search and rescue is done by survivors, not external teams

Importance of socioeconomic factors in effects of disaster

Characteristics and effects of earthquake	San Fernando, California, 1971	Managua, Nicaragua, 1972
Magnitude (Richter scale)	6.6	5.6
Duration of strong shaking (seconds)	10	5-10
Population of affected area	7 000 000	420 000
No of deaths	60	4 000-6 000
No of people injured	2 540	20 000
No of houses destroyed or unsafe	915	50 000

Adapted from Seaman J. *Epidemiology of natural disasters.* Basel: Karger, 1984

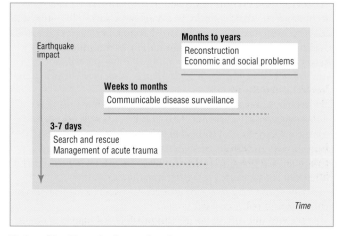
Timing of health needs after earthquake

Buildings and injury from earthquake

- Multistorey framed construction leaves cavities in a "lean to" or "tent" collapse where minimally injured survivors may be found
- Medium and low rise buildings of brick or local materials collapse into rubble with little or no room for survivors
- Residential property is more fully occupied at night, when earthquakes can be more deadly

Risks associated with entrapment after an earthquake

- Lack of oxygen
- Hypothermia
- Gas leak
- Smoke
- Water penetration
- Electrocution

Up to three times as many people are injured as are killed, presenting an enormous burden to local medical facilities. The combination of injury and entrapment places a limit on survival. Major head and chest injuries are usually fatal. Peripheral limb injuries are the commonest surgical problems, and the effects of crush injury are the most complex.

The greatest effects of earthquakes will be non-medical, with the loss of communication, transport, and power. Water supplies can be disrupted but are rarely contaminated. Fear of the unburied dead as a reservoir for disease is unfounded.

Tsunami (tidal wave)

Earthquakes occurring at sea may produce seismic waves; as these Tsunami approach land and enter shallower water, they slow and the energy transfers into a wall of water. Buildings are destroyed by the initial impact, and by the drag of water returning to the sea eroding foundations. Further danger comes from residual flooding and floating debris. Most deaths are due to drowning, and, unlike in earthquakes, the dead outnumber the injured. This was vividly shown by the tsunami in the Indian Ocean on 26 December 2004.

Landslides

Heavy storms can destabilise rock and soil, particularly in areas of deforestation (a human made rather than natural phenomenon). Mudflows can follow tsunami, floods, and occasionally earthquakes. Extricating victims from the compressive effect of the mud can be difficult, and the weight of the mud can produce crush injury and crush syndrome. Intravenous fluid loading before, during, and after rescue may protect against a catastrophic fall in blood pressure that can follow sudden release after prolonged entrapment.

Floods

Although the immediate impact on survivors is likely to be injury and the death of relatives, damage to crops, housing, and infrastructure can conspire to precipitate acute food shortages and homelessness. Water supplies may be contaminated with sewage, leading to disease.

Volcanic eruptions

Because volcanic ash eventually provides highly fertile soil, areas vulnerable to volcanic activity are often well populated. There is a greater risk from injury from falling rocks than there is from burns, but homelessness, both temporary and permanent, poses the biggest threat to health. Special threats to life include ash falls, pyroclastic flows (horizontal blasts of gas containing ash and larger fragments in suspension), mud flows, tsunami, and volcanic earthquake.

Hot volcanic ash in the air can produce inhalational burns, but only superficial burns to the upper airways will be survived. Respiratory effects of ash include excessive mucus production with obstructive mucus plugs, acute respiratory distress syndrome, asphyxia, exacerbation of asthma, and silicosis. Toxic gases may be emitted, and poisoning from carbon monoxide, hydrofluoric acid, and sulphur dioxide can occur.

Tropical storms

Convention dictates that tropical storms in the Indian Ocean are called cyclones, those in the north Atlantic, Caribbean, and south Pacific are called hurricanes, and those in the north and west Pacific are called typhoons. They occur as humid air twists upwards from warm sea water into cooler air above. Over the sea, air may move at speeds of more than 300 kph, twisting anticlockwise in the northern hemisphere and clockwise in the southern. Flying debris causes injury, and secondary flooding may occur.

Aftermath of the 1988 Armenian earthquake. The unburied dead pose little or no risk to the living

---

Crush injury and crush syndrome

Crush injury	Crush syndrome
• Skin necrosis	• Rhabdomyolysis
• Rhabdomyolysis	• Renal failure
• Bony injury	• Hyperkalaemia

Volcanic eruption, Cape Verde. The eruption itself caused few deaths and injuries, but a cholera outbreak followed the mass evacuation of local people to tented accommodation

---

Dangers from volcanic eruptions

Lava flows
- Destroy everything in their path
- Risk of secondary fires
- Move slowly and predictably
- Limited direct risk to life

Pyroclastic flows
- Horizontal blasts of gas containing ash and larger fragments in suspension
- Material can be 1000°C
- Move at several hundred kph
- Speed and unpredictability of movement pose a considerable risk to life

Mudflows
- Occur when heavy rain emulsifies ash and loose volcanic material
- The mud, with a consistency of wet concrete, can reach speeds > 100 kph flowing downhill

Famine

Famine may complicate all "natural" and human made disasters, and socioeconomic and political issues lie at the roots of cause and prevention. Trigger levels for urgent humanitarian intervention include a rise in crude mortality to 1 in 10 000 a day, pronounced wasting (loss of $> 15\%$ of normal body weight), and food energy supplies of < 1500 kcal (6.3 MJ) a day.

An adequate response requires planning and coordination at national and international levels. Famine, like other "natural disasters," leads to the mass movement of people. It is a cause or consequence of other humanitarian crises including complex emergencies—where conflict compounds humanitarian needs and responses.

Children are among the most vulnerable during famine

Case study

Hurricane Andrew and health coordination

Three days after Hurricane Andrew struck south Florida in August 1992, epidemiologists performed a rapid needs assessment using a modified cluster sampling method. Firstly, clusters were systematically selected from a heavily damaged area by using a grid laid over aerial photographs. Survey teams interviewed seven occupied households in each selected cluster. Surveys of the same area and of a less severely affected area were conducted seven and 10 days later, respectively.

Initial results, available within 24 hours of starting the survey, found few injured residents but many households without working telephones or electricity. Relief workers were then able to focus on providing primary care and preventive services rather than diverting resources towards unnecessary mass casualty services. This represented the first use of cluster surveys to obtain population based data after a natural disaster (previously they had been used in refugee camps to assess nutritional and health status).

Medical services were severely affected: acute care facilities and community health centres were closed, and doctors' offices destroyed. State and federal public health officials, the American Red Cross, and the military established temporary medical facilities. Within four weeks after the hurricane, officials established disease surveillance facilities at civilian and military centres providing free care and at emergency departments in and around the disaster area. Public health workers reviewed medical logbooks and patient records daily, and recorded the number of patient visits using simple diagnostic categories (such as diarrhoea, cough, rash).

This surveillance allowed the health status of the affected population to be characterised and the effectiveness of emergency public health measures to be evaluated. Surveillance information was particularly useful in refuting rumours about epidemics, so avoiding widespread use of typhoid vaccine, and in showing that large numbers of volunteer healthcare providers were not needed.

Although the surveillance achieved its objectives, there were several problems. Data from the civilian and military systems had to be analysed separately because different case definitions and data collection methods were used. There was no baseline information available to determine whether health events were occurring more frequently than expected. Also, rates of illness and injury could not be determined for civilians because the size of the population at risk was unknown.

Although proportional morbidity (number of visits for each cause divided by the total number of visits) can be easily obtained, it is often difficult to interpret. An increase in one category (such as respiratory illness) may result from a decline in another category (such as injuries) rather than from a true increase in the incidence of respiratory illness.

Hurricane Andrew, one of the most destructive hurricanes in US history, inflicted widespread damage

Further reading

- Pan American Health Organisation (PAHO). www.paho.org/disasters
- Centre for Disease Control and Prevention. Natural disasters and severe weather. www.bt.cdc.gov/disasters
- Hogan DE, Burstein JL. *Disaster Medicine*. London: Lippincott Williams and Wilkins, 2002
- Ryan JM, Mahoney PF, Greaves I, Bowyer G, eds. *Conflict and catastrophe medicine: a practical guide*. London: Springer-Verlag, 2002
- Sphere Project. *Humanitarian charter and minimum standards in disaster response*. Geneva: Sphere Project, 2004. www.sphereproject.org

The case study of Hurricane Andrew and health coordination was supplied by Eric K Noji, senior medical officer, Centers for Disease Control and Prevention, Washington Office, USA. The picture showing damage from Hurricane Andrew was taken by Bob Epstein and supplied by the Federal Emergency Management Agency (FEMA).

Competing interests: None declared.

3 Needs assessment of humanitarian crises

Anthony D Redmond

As many as two billion people are at risk of or exposed to crisis conditions, and some 20 million people live in such conditions. Communities are exposed to crisis conditions when local and national systems are overwhelmed and are unable to meet their basic needs. This may be because of a sudden increase in demand (when food and water are in short supply) or because the institutions that support communities are weak (when government and local services collapse because of staff shortages or lack of funds).

Crises can be triggered by:
- Sudden, catastrophic events—such as earthquakes, hurricanes, flooding, or industrial incidents
- Complex, continuing emergencies—including the 100 or so conflicts currently under way, and the many millions of people displaced as a result
- Slow onset disasters—such as widespread arsenic poisoning in the Ganges delta, the increasing prevalence of HIV infection and AIDS, or economic collapse.

Triage of patients in a refugee camp on the Iran-Iraq border

Importance of needs assessment

The immediate global reporting of crises can and often does provoke cries of "Something must be done." Laudable as such sentiments might be, if that something is not what is needed, its uninvited dispatch can only divert already stretched human and physical resources away from the task in hand.

If aid is to do the most good for the most people it must be targeted. To do this, a rapid needs assessment should be carried out as soon as possible and in direct consultation with local authorities. The resuscitation of a population is similar to the resuscitation of a severely injured patient, with needs assessment as the all important primary survey.

Those making the assessments should be experienced and recognised as acting on behalf of international agencies. However, too many assessments can waste time, unnecessarily duplicate effort, and frustrate the host community. Sharing and comparing information allows a clearer and more consistent picture to emerge, and smaller agencies can increase the speed and relevance of their response by referring to the reports of large international agencies and browsing relevant websites.

Whatever is done at the start must shorten and not prolong the recovery period and, most importantly, not increase dependency. Without attention to the local economy, food aid can destroy the local market and wipe out self sufficiency. If donated equipment is unfamiliar or cannot be maintained locally, its impact and useful life are limited and its introduction is more likely to devalue and undermine local practice than to support it.

The nature of the disaster

The type of incident will determine the scale and type of consequences. For example, earthquakes and landslides cause crush injuries, and volcanoes cause breathing problems. All large scale incidents, but particularly conflicts, create the mass movement of people. The geography, climate, and weather will determine physical access to the disaster area. Political instability will influence the feasibility of the humanitarian response.

Homeless survivors of earthquake

> A United Nations disaster assessment and coordination (UNDAC) team is a two to six person team drawn from member countries that travels quickly to a disaster scene to report the immediate needs to the international community

The assessment team

- The team must be self sufficient in food, water, shelter, medical supplies, transport, and communications
- A practical team size is often two to six people, splitting into teams of two once in the country
- While one assessor does the talking, a companion listens, observes, and takes notes. In this way little is missed or misinterpreted

The impact of the disaster

The number of people killed immediately by an event is an obvious measure of its impact. However, the number of survivors is more important. When subsequent death rates are measured, the number should be compared with the international standard of one death per 10 000 population per day.

Close attention should be paid to the most vulnerable groups, particularly children, whose health will provide early warning of any growing threat. When communicating need, highlight the needs of the most vulnerable first.

Prioritising needs

Although the medical needs of the affected population might seem to be the most pressing issue, lack of non-medical necessities is usually the most immediate threat to life.

Drinking water—People die of thirst long before they starve. The greatest immediate threat is always lack of adequate drinking water. Because humans require so much water, its quality must be balanced against its quantity: an adequate quantity of reasonably safe water is preferable to a smaller quantity of pure water. For most aspects of emergency relief, it is important to avoid "temporary" holding measures, which often fail to be replaced and become inadequate longer term measures. However, the urgency of supplying water is so great that temporary systems to meet immediate needs must often be installed, to be improved or replaced later.

Sanitation—After water, the greatest need is for sanitation. Once again, pragmatism dictates that the swift provision of a basic system will save more lives than the delayed provision of a perfect system. Ensure there is at least one latrine seat for every 20 people and that each dwelling is no more than one minute's walk from a toilet. For every 500 people there must be at least one communal refuse pit measuring 2 m × 5 m × 2 m.

Food—The minimum maintenance level of food energy intake is accepted internationally as 2100 kcal (8.8 MJ) per person per day. When this falls below 1500 kcal (6.3 MJ) a day mortality rises rapidly in populations already stressed. Locally prepared food with local ingredients is best received and therefore of greatest use. Moreover, the purchase of local ingredients by local and international agencies supports the local economy and is sustainable. If food cannot be obtained locally then the provision of dried imported food still allows local preparation.

Shelter—The effects on social infrastructure, particularly housing, must be assessed at an early stage and permanent shelter established as soon as possible. "Temporary housing" is rarely replaced and should be avoided. The minimum floor area for a human to live in dignity is 3.5 m² per person. Clothing is often sent to stricken areas, but its transport is expensive and its storage can be difficult and costly. Financial support to larger agencies is usually the better way of addressing such needs.

Medical needs—The most important medical issues will be infectious diseases. Children younger than 5 years are most vulnerable. Foreign emergency medical aid is often required, but usually in the form of materials rather than people. World Health Organization emergency health kits can be dispatched quickly and are available to match populations of varying size. Although primary care needs are paramount, limited support to secondary care is sometimes appropriate.

International search and rescue teams—The publicity such teams attract can mask their limitations, and their uninvited arrival diverts precious resources. Remember that the survivors of a disaster provide most rescue effort and that survival from entrapment declines rapidly after 24-36 hours. The times when

Assessing a disaster by mortality*

Adults and children aged ≥5 years		Children aged <5 years	
≤ 1	Under control	≤ 1	"Normal" in a developing country
> 1	Serious condition	< 2	Emergency under control
> 2	Out of control	> 2	Emergency in serious trouble
> 4	Major catastrophe	> 4	Emergency out of control

*Mortality per 10 000 population per day

Material aid should be targeted on identified needs

Requirements for an emergency water supply

- Minimum maintenance requirements (including hygiene needs) are 15-20 litres per person each day
- A feeding centre should aim to provide 20-30 l/person/day and a health centre to provide 40-60 l/person/day
- Safe storage should be provided near to homes

Assessing malnutrition in children aged under 5 years

- Middle upper arm circumference (MUAC) is a rough guide to nutritional status: normal > 14.0 cm, severe malnutrition < 11.0 cm, moderate malnutrition 11.0-13.5 cm
- A malnutrition emergency is when > 10% of children are moderately malnourished
- Weight for height ratio (z score) is more accurate than MUAC but is more complex to calculate

---

Trigger levels for urgent action

Rise in mortality
- Crude mortality > 1/10 000/day
- Mortality in children aged < 5 years > 4/10 000/day

Fall in energy supply
- < 1500 kcal/day in adults
- < 100 kcal/kg/day in infants and small children
- Reduced z score or MUAC in 10% of children aged < 5 years
- Wasting > 15% of normal body weight

Common infectious diseases associated with disasters

- Acute respiratory infections
- Cholera
- Other diarrhoeal diseases
- Measles
- Malaria
- Meningitis

WHO emergency health kits

- Basic and supplementary units available
- Each unit intended to assist a population of 10 000 for 3 months
- Entire unit fits on back of standard pick up truck
- Basic unit
  Weighs 45 kg, 0.2 m³ in size
  Contains only oral drugs
  Meant for primary health workers
- Supplementary unit
  Weighs 410 kg, 2 m³ in size
  For sole use of health professionals
  Does not duplicate basic unit and cannot be used alone

international search and rescue teams might be needed are when:

- A large urban area has been affected
- Buildings of more than two stories have collapsed
- Collapsed buildings may have left spaces where victims could survive
- Local facilities are inadequate.

Assessment of existing response

Local response

The impact of the disaster on a community is the product of the number of people affected minus their ability and capacity to cope. Quickly establish what the situation was like before the crisis; if necessary assess an unaffected area. Find a familiar point of reference; hospitals can provide a reasonable reflection of the wider community and are often readily accessible to those with a medical background and experience.

Identify what has been done so far and what immediate inputs would be of greatest help to local efforts. Identify key local players and direct any aid workers who follow you to the local authorities.

Try to distinguish between emergency and chronic needs. Support what local structure exists, as imposing foreign organisational structures is ineffective and indeed destructive in a crisis.

International response

Establish which international agencies are already at the scene and which are expected. Competition is wasteful, so encourage cooperation between agencies and the sharing of information. Encourage and support the local authorities to establish and run a coordination centre for international relief agencies. The WHO and United Nations are usually best placed to liase between local government and relief agencies. UN disaster assessment and coordination (UNDAC) teams now try to establish an on site operations and coordination centre for this purpose. Coordination and cooperation are the keys to maximising the international effort.

Making recommendations

Logistics—Whatever you recommend will be sent to those in need only if it can be procured, dispatched, and delivered on time. Assess the status and capacity of airports, seaports, and roads and the availability of trucks and drivers.

Future developments—Find out what the local authorities plan to do next. Support the development of a clear strategy and encourage outside agencies to conform to and work within this framework.

Setting priorities—When identifying needs, clarify which are immediate, which are medium term, and which are longer term.

Although the urge to give "things" and send people can be powerful, cash contributions will often best support the local economy by the purchase of local goods and materials. Remember, a recommendation to do nothing, either at all or at the present moment, can be a valid and helpful conclusion. If the local community is coping, the inappropriate or untimely dispatch of aid can add to, rather than relieve, the burden of the affected country.

The WHO, Department for Health Action in Crises, Geneva, Switzerland, contributed to the writing of this article.

Competing interests: None declared.

Unrequested and inappropriate aid left abandoned at a local airfield

Key tasks for WHO in response to humanitarian crises

- Assessment and analysis, anticipation and forecasting
- Coordination of relief agencies involved
- Identifying gaps in preparation and response
- Helping strengthen local capacity to prepare for and deal with crises

Making recommendations for humanitarian aid

- Identify the level and type of assistance required
- Give a timescale
- Clarify whether the need is for people or materials
- Keep it simple
- Support the local economic structure
- Ensure sustainability

Issues to be addressed in evaluations of refugee health programmes

- Appropriateness and cost effectiveness of the response
- Coverage and coherence of the response
- Connectedness and impact of the response

Further reading

- World Health Organization. www.who.int
- OCHA (United Nations Office for the Coordination of Humanitarian Affairs) ochaonline.un.org
- World Health Organization. *Rapid health assessment protocols for emergencies.* Geneva: WHO, 1999
- Leaning J, Briggs SM, Chen LC. Eds. *Humanitarian crises: the medical and public health response.* Boston: Harvard University Press, 1999
- Pan American Health Organization and World Health Organization. *Humanitarian supply management and logistics in the health sector.* Washington DC: PAHO and WHO, 2001. www.paho.org/english/ped/supplies.htm

4 Public health in the aftermath of disasters

Eric K Noji

In the aftermath of disasters, public health services must address the effects of civil strife, armed conflict, population migration, economic collapse, and famine. In modern conflicts civilians are targeted deliberately, and affected populations may face severe public health consequences, even without displacement from their homes. For displaced people, damage to health, sanitation, water supplies, housing, and agriculture may lead to a rapid increase in malnutrition and communicable diseases.

Fortunately, the provision of adequate clean water and sanitation, timely measles immunisation, simple treatment of dehydration from diarrhoea, supplementary feeding for the malnourished, micronutrient supplements, and the establishment of an adequate public health surveillance system greatly reduces the health risks associated with the harsh environments of refugee camps.

Critical public health interventions

Environmental health
Overcrowding, inadequate hygiene and sanitation, and the resulting poor water supplies increase the incidence of diarrhoea, malaria, respiratory infections, measles, and other communicable diseases. A good system of water supply and excreta disposal must be put in place quickly. No amount of curative health measures can offset the harmful effects of poor environmental health planning for communities in emergency settlements. Where camps are unavoidable, appropriate site location and layout and spacing and type of shelter can mitigate the conditions that lead to the spread of disease.

Water supply and sanitation
Adequate sources of potable water and sanitation (collection, disposal, and treatment of excreta and other liquid and solid wastes) must be equally accessible for all camp residents. This is achieved by installing an appropriate number of suitably located waste disposal facilities (toilets, latrines, defecation fields, or solid waste pick-up points), water distribution points, availability of soap and bathing and washing facilities, and effective health education.

The United Nations High Commissioner for Refugees (UNHCR) recommends that each refugee receive a minimum of 15-20 litres of clean water per day for domestic needs. Adequate quantities of relatively clean water are preferable to small amounts of high quality water. Provision of lidded buckets to each family, chlorinated just before they are distributed and again each time they are refilled, is a labour intensive but effective preventive measure that can be instituted early in an emergency.

Latrine construction should begin early in the acute phase of an emergency, but initial sanitation measures in a camp may be nothing more than designating an area for defecation that is segregated from the source of potable water. Construction of one latrine for every 20 people is recommended.

Vector control
The control of disease vectors (mosquitoes, flies, rats, and fleas) is a critical environmental health measure.

The Indonesian city of Banda Ache, Sumatra, after the devastating tsunami on 26 December 2004

Priorities for a coordinated health programme for emergency settlements

- Protection from natural and human hazards
- Census or registration systems
- Adequate quantities of reasonably clean water
- Acceptable foods with recommended nutrient and energy composition
  Where it is difficult to ensure that vulnerable groups have access to rations or where high rates of malnutrition exist, supplementary feeding programmes should be established
- Adequate shelter
- Well functioning and culturally appropriate sanitation and hygiene systems (such as latrines and buckets, chlorine and soap)
- Family tracing (essential for mental health)
- Information and coordination with other vital sectors such as food, transport, communication, and housing monitoring and evaluation, for prompt problem solving
- Medical and health services

Survivors of the tsunami in Meulaboh, Sumatra, crowd around a US Navy helicopter delivering food and water. Helicopter was often the only means of reaching the worst affected regions

Shelter
The World Health Organization recommends 30 m² of living space per person—plus the necessary land for communal activities, agriculture, and livestock—as a minimum overall figure for planning a camp layout. Of this total living space, 3.5 m² is the absolute minimum floor space per person in emergency shelters.

Communicable disease control and epidemic management
Malnutrition, diarrhoeal diseases, measles, acute respiratory infections, and malaria consistently account for 60-95% of reported deaths among refugees and displaced populations. Preventing high mortality from communicable disease epidemics in displaced populations relies primarily on the prompt provision of adequate quantities of water, basic sanitation, community outreach, and effective case management of ill patients allied to essential drugs and public health surveillance to trigger early appropriate control measures. Proper management of diarrhoeal diseases with relatively simple, low technology measures can reduce case fatality to less than 1%, even in cholera epidemics.

Immunisation
Immunisation of children against measles is one of the most important (and cost effective) preventive measures in affected populations, particularly those housed in camps. Since infants as young as 6 months old often contract measles in refugee camp outbreaks and are at increased risk of dying because of impaired nutrition, measles immunisation programmes (along with vitamin A supplements) are recommended in emergency settings for all children from the ages of 6 months to 5 years (some would recommend up to 12-14 years). Ideally, measles immunisation coverage in refugee camps should be greater than 80%. Immunisation programmes should eventually include all antigens recommended by WHO's expanded programme on immunisation (EPI).

Controlling the spread of HIV/AIDS
The massive threat posed by HIV infection and allied sexually transmitted diseases, such as syphilis, is exacerbated by civil conflict and disasters. HIV spreads fastest during emergencies, when conditions such as poverty, powerlessness, social instability, and violence against women are most extreme. Moreover, during complex emergencies control activities, whether undertaken by national governments or by other international and national agencies, tend to be disrupted or break down altogether.

Education, health, poverty, human rights and legal issues, forced migration and refugees, security, military forces, and violence against women are only some of the factors related to HIV transmission that must be considered. The *Guidelines for HIV/AIDS interventions in emergency settings*, elaborated by WHO, UNHCR, and UNAIDS Joint United Nations Programme on HIV/AIDS, is an important resource and must be disseminated and implemented in the field.

Management of dead bodies
One of the commonest myths associated with disasters is that cadavers represent a serious threat of epidemics. This is used as justification for widespread and inappropriate mass burial or cremation of victims. As well as being scientifically unfounded, this practice leads to serious breaches of the principle of human dignity, depriving families of their right to know something about their missing relatives. It is urgent to stop propagating such disaster myths and obtain global consensus on the appropriate management of dead bodies after disasters.

Tents erected to accommodate the local population displaced by a volcanic eruption in Cape Verde. Such mass movement of people into temporary accommodation can pose the greatest threat to life after a disaster: in this case a cholera outbreak developed

Factors influencing disease transmission after disasters

- Pre-existing disease (such as cholera, measles, typhus)
- Immunisation rates
- Concentration of population
- Damage to utilities, contamination of water or food
- Increased disease transmission by vectors—breeding sites, lack of personal hygiene, interruption of control programmes

Uniforms of the Naval Environmental Preventive Medicine Unit being sprayed with mosquito repellent in preparation for deployment to Indonesia to help the humanitarian effort. The unit provides water quality testing, bug spraying, and treatment of illnesses in the tsunami survivors

Ten critical emergency relief measures

- Rapidly assess the health status of the affected population
- Establish disease surveillance and a health information system
- Immunise all children aged 6 months to 5 years against measles and provide vitamin A to those with malnutrition
- Institute diarrhoea control programmes
- Provide elementary sanitation and clean water
- Provide adequate shelters, clothes, and blankets
- Ensure at least 1900 kcal of food per person per day
- Establish curative services with standard treatment protocols based on essential drug lists that provide basic coverage to entire community
- Organise human resources to ensure one community health expert per 1000 population
- Coordinate activities of local authorities, national agencies, international agencies, and non-governmental organisations

Nutrition

Undernutrition increases the case mortality from measles, diarrhoea, and other infectious diseases. Deficiencies of vitamins A and C have been associated with increased childhood mortality in non-refugee populations. Because malnutrition contributes greatly to overall refugee morbidity and mortality, nutritional rehabilitation and maintenance of adequate nutritional levels can be among the most effective interventions (along with measles immunisation) to decrease mortality, particularly for such vulnerable groups as pregnant women, breast feeding mothers, young children, handicapped people, and elderly people. However, the highest nutritional priority in refugee camps is the timely provision of general food rations containing ideally 2100 kcal (8.8 MJ) per person per day and that include sufficient protein, fat, and micronutrients.

Maternal and child health (including reproductive health)

Maternal deaths have been shown to account for a substantial burden of mortality among refugee women of reproductive age. Maternal and child healthcare programmes may include health education and outreach; prenatal, delivery, and postnatal care; nutritional supplementation; encouragement of breast feeding; family planning and preventing spread of sexually transmitted diseases and HIV; and immunisation and weight monitoring for infants. Giving women who are heads of households the responsibility for distribution of relief supplies, particularly food, ensures more equitable allocation of relief items.

Medical services

Experience shows that medical care in emergency situations should be based on simple, standardised protocols. Conveniently accessible primary health clinics should be established at the start of the emergency phase. WHO and other organisations, such as Médecins Sans Frontières, have developed basic, field tested protocols for managing common clinical problems that are easily adaptable for emergency situations. Underlying these basic case management protocols are what have been termed "essential" drug and supply lists. Such standard treatment protocols and basic supplies are designed to help health workers (most of whom will be non-physicians) provide appropriate curative care and allow the most efficient use of limited resources.

Public health surveillance

Emergency health information systems are now routinely established to monitor the health of populations affected by complex humanitarian emergencies. Crude mortality is the most critical indicator of a population's improving or deteriorating health status and is the indicator to which donors and relief agencies most readily respond. It not only indicates the current health state of a population but also provides a baseline against which the effectiveness of relief programmes can be measured. During the emergency phase of a relief operation, mortality should be expressed as deaths/10 000/day to allow for detection of sudden changes. In general, health workers should be extremely concerned when mortality in a displaced population exceeds 1/10 000/day or when it exceeds 4/10 000/day in children aged less than 5 years old.

The photographs of Banda Ache, Meulaboh, and of uniform spraying were supplied by the US Navy and were taken by Photographer's Mate Airman Patrick M. Bonafede, Photographer's Mate Airman Jordon R Beesley, and Photographer's Mate Second Class Jennifer L Bailey respectively. The photographs of nutritional assessment in Somalia were supplied by Brent Burkholder, Centers for Disease Control and Prevention.

Competing interests: None declared.

Nutritional assessment team in refugee camp, Somalia, 1993 (left) and use of Salter scales to determine protein energy malnutrition ("wasting") in young child (right)

Emergency health clinic run by Liberian Red Cross for citizens displaced by renewed civil war in downtown Monrovia, Liberia, 1996

Further reading

- Perrin P. *Handbook on war and public health*. Geneva: International Committee of the Red Cross, 1996
- Centers for Disease Control. Famine-affected, refugee, and displaced populations: recommendations for public health issues. *MMWR Recomm Rep* 1992;41(RR-13):1-76
- Noji EK, ed. *The public health consequences of disasters*. Oxford: Oxford University Press, 1997
- Pan American Health Organization. *Natural disasters: protecting the public's health*. Washington DC: PAHO, 2000
- World Health Organization. *Rapid health assessment protocols for emergencies*. Geneva: WHO, 1999
- World Health Organization. *The management of nutrition in major emergencies*. Geneva: WHO, 2000
- Médecins Sans Frontières. *Refugee health: an approach to emergency situations*. Paris: MSF, 1997
- Sphere Project. *Humanitarian charter and minimum standards in disaster response*. Geneva: Sphere Project, 2004. www.sphereproject.org

5 Military approach to medical planning in humanitarian operations

Martin C M Bricknell, Tracey MacCormack

Military medical forces may be the only medical services available in the immediate aftermath of conflict and are often required to coordinate the re-establishment of civilian services. UK military medical services have a long history of providing assistance in humanitarian emergencies.

Military medical planners apply a structured approach to determine the requirements for medical support to military operations. This "medical estimate" has two outputs. The first develops health promotion and preventive medicine advice and actions to help maintain the physical, psychological, and social health of the military force. The second output develops missions and tasks for the medical elements of the force.

Estimate format

In military medical planning, a planner is given a mission by headquarters. The planner is required to assess this mission to establish missions for his or her subordinates. If the mission is unclear the planner may seek further information from intelligence reports or reconnaissance. Thus, the critical task is interpretation of the mission in order to give subordinates instructions to fulfil the planner's interpretation of the problem.

Background information—At the start of an estimate it is important to assemble background information. This might include maps, situation reports for the local area, news reports, and information about prevalent diseases. Internet sites hosted by international aid organisations such as the United Nations, World Health Organization, US Centers for Disease Control, and the UK Health Protection Agency may contain useful information. Less formal sites such as ReliefWeb and Well Diggers Workstation contain much practical information.

The steps in the estimate

An estimate follows five steps: mission analysis, evaluation of factors, consideration of courses of action, commander's decision, and development of the plan.

Step 1: Mission analysis
An estimate starts with a mission analysis based on the mission statement provided by headquarters. Ideally, this mission statement should be a unifying task with a purpose similar to that of a vision statement in management. Mission analysis involves interpreting the mission to deduce the tasks specified in the mission and those that are implied.

Step 2: Evaluation of factors
This step is designed as a series of tools and checklists to enable the medical planner to determine "how to do it." Its structured format is designed to allow an estimate to be made by a single individual or by several planners working on separate aspects.

Environment—The geography of the area of operation is reviewed, and factors such as distance, environmental temperature, roads, airfields, and other geographical features are considered. The locations of indigenous medical facilities and structures such as water treatment facilities, power stations, food storage sites, etc, must be noted.

British Army ambulance in a refugee camp in Kosovo, 1999. Military medical forces may be the only medical services available in the immediate aftermath of conflict

---

The five steps of the military medical estimate

Step 1—Mission analysis

Step 2—Evaluation of factors
General factors—environment, friendly forces, hostile forces, surprise, security, time
Medical factors—casualty estimate; medical logistics; medical facilities and capabilities; medical force protection; nuclear, biological, and chemical defence; medical "C4" (command and control, communications and computers)
Humanitarian factors—the 10 priorities of Médecins Sans Frontières

Step 3—Consideration of courses of action

Step 4—Commander's decision

Step 5—Implementing the plan

Examples of mission statements given to military medical forces in humanitarian operations

Kurdistan 1991
To assist in the provision of security and humanitarian assistance in order to expedite the movement of Kurdish displaced persons from refugee camps directly to their homes

Rwanda 1994
To provide humanitarian assistance in the south west of Rwanda in order to encourage the refugee population to stay in that part of the country

---

Senior military medical planners and commanders discussing medical arrangements to support military exercise SAIF SERREA in Oman, 2001

Hostile forces—Medical planners should review the weapons available to hostile forces (small arms, artillery or aircraft, mines, booby traps, etc) to generate a list of the types of injuries that might need treatment. The threat from release of chemicals (either deliberately or from collateral damage to industrial facilities) should be identified at this stage. Indigenous diseases are also considered as hostile forces.

Friendly forces and the population at risk—It is vital to know how many people are dependent on the health service plan— the population at risk. In humanitarian operations this often comprises two groups, providers and recipients of the humanitarian response.

Casualty estimate—This requires assessment of hostile forces and friendly forces to produce an estimate of the numbers and types of casualties that will require treatment and evacuation.

Security—Combatants in complex humanitarian emergencies increasingly regard the humanitarian community, including medical workers, as targets. It is vital that the security of the humanitarian community be given a high priority. This has to be balanced against the constraints it places on humanitarian workers' ability to meet the needs of the dependent population.

Medical force protection—This identifies the preventive medical actions that need to be taken to protect both the humanitarian community and the dependent community from threats identified from hostile forces. Examples might include pre-deployment immunisation, security of food and water sources to prevent gastrointestinal illness, measures to prevent insect bites and chemoprophylaxis against malaria, and use of body armour to protect against fragmentation weapons.

Time—Ideally, the organisation of ambulance services and the location of medical facilities should minimise delays in the provision of care. Such considerations must, however, be balanced against the resources available and the need to maintain the security of medical staff.

Medical capabilities—Review of the preceding factors will determine the capabilities and capacity of each medical facility required (surgical, paediatric, environmental health).

Medical logistics—Medical logistics merits a separate heading because of the technical complexity of the subject. Detailed planning for supply of individual items—such as oxygen, clinical waste disposal, and blood and blood products—needs to be considered in addition to planning for medical treatments. Special attention must be paid to the storage and distribution chain to ensure that medical material is kept within specified temperatures.

Medical C4—The medical system's efficiency depends on the effectiveness of the "C4" (command and control, communications and computers) of the various medical elements. The treatment and movement of a single casualty may require coordination of several medical facilities and organisations. It may be necessary to establish liaison officers, communication links, and other means of passing information efficiently between medical agencies involved in the humanitarian response.

Humanitarian factors—Médecins Sans Frontières recommend 10 priorities for intervention. The relative importance of these priorities will depend on the exact humanitarian emergency. The forced displacement in a Balkan winter of previously well fed and healthy civilians will create different challenges to those arising from severe flooding affecting a malnourished population with endemic malaria in Mozambique. The principal task is assessment. Various information gathering tools are available for humanitarian emergencies. Ideally, the humanitarian community should rapidly establish a common system for data collection so that all agencies can contribute to initial assessment and collation into a shared database.

A review of the weapons available to hostile forces will indicate the types of injury that might need treatment

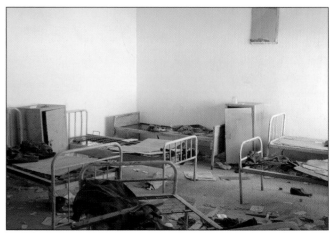

A looted hospital ward in Iraq in 2003, showing the need for adequate protection of medical forces

Main medical warehouse in Basra, Iraq, after delivery of a major humanitarian aid shipment in 2003. The technical complexity of medical logistics means it requires careful and detailed consideration

---

Médecins Sans Frontières' 10 priorities for medical intervention in humanitarian emergencies

1—Initial assessment	6—Health care in the emergency phase
2—Measles immunisation	7—Control of communicable disease and epidemics
3—Water and sanitation	
4—Food and nutrition	8—Public health surveillance
5—Shelter and site planning	9—Human resources and training
	10—Coordination

Assessment of tasks—The evaluation of factors will generate a list of tasks. These should be listed and matched to resources.

Step 3: Consideration of courses of action
This is often the most difficult but most important step of the medical estimate. The tasks generated in step 2 must be converted into a series of mission statements or task lists for the medical elements of the military force. Ideally, the estimate process will lead to a list of key tasks, some of which may have various options.

Step 4: Commander's decision
During military action, the commanding officer will have the final accountability for the medical plan. In a multiagency humanitarian response it will be necessary to spend much energy in generating consensus for any plan. Although military medical staff have well developed planning and decision making skills, it may be more appropriate for other agencies to take the lead in planning and coordinating the healthcare response.

Step 5: Development of the plan
A plan has no value unless it can be communicated to and coordinated by all parties involved. This may require written instructions and verbal briefings. Each humanitarian agency may have its own similar procedures. As an estimate starts with mission analysis, the medical planner must carefully craft the "mission statements" for each of the component parts of the medical response so that the subordinate leaders understand how their missions contribute to the overall humanitarian response and are able to conduct their own medical estimates.

Graphical tools such as marked maps or project planning timetables may help to convey specific details. Planning conferences and workshops, such as tabletop exercises used in emergency planning, may also help mutual understanding between organisations.

Written instructions and verbal briefings may be needed as the medical planner assigns each of the component parts of the military medical response to subordinate leaders

The final military medical plan must be aligned to the overall humanitarian plan for the affected region

Summary

The military medical estimate is a formal decision making tool. It provides a structure to allow analysis of the factors involved in complex humanitarian emergencies. The output of the estimate is a plan for the military medical response to a humanitarian crisis. The estimate may provide a suitable structure for use by other organisations working in similar environments.

The medical plan must be aligned to the overall humanitarian plan. This often considers wider humanitarian issues such as security; law and order; food, water, and fuel distribution; establishment of representative government; education; and other developmental issues.

Competing interests: None declared.

Further reading
- Médecins Sans Frontières. *Refugee health. An approach to emergency situations.* London: MacMillan Education, 1997
- World Health Organization. *Rapid health assessment protocols for emergencies.* Geneva: WHO,1999
- UN Office for the Coordination of Humanitarian Affairs Military and Civil Defence Unit. *Guidelines on the use of military and civil defence assets to support United Nations humanitarian activities in complex emergencies.* Geneva: MCDU, 2003.
- Roberts L. *Staying alive: safety and security guidelines for humanitarian volunteers in conflict areas.* Geneva: ICRC Publications, 1999
- De Lorenzo R, Porter RS. *Tactical emergency care: military and operational out of hospital medicine.* London: Brady Prentice Hall, 1999

6 Principles of war surgery

Steve J Mannion, Eddie Chaloner

Managing war injury is no longer the exclusive preserve of military surgeons. Increasing numbers of non-combatants are injured in modern conflicts, and peacetime surgical facilities and expertise may not be available. This article addresses the management of war wounds by non-specialist surgeons with limited resources and expertise. One of the hallmarks of war injury is the early lethality of wounds to the head, chest, and abdomen; therefore, limb injuries form a high proportion of the wounds that present at hospitals during conflicts.

Wounding patterns

Gunshot wounds

The incidence of gunshot wounds in conflict depends on the type and intensity of the fighting. In full scale war the proportion of casualties injured by gunshot is generally less than in low intensity or asymmetric warfare.

Bullets cause injury by:
- Direct laceration of vital structures
- Stretching of tissue (cavitation), causing fracturing of blood vessels and devitalisation of tissue
- Secondary contamination.

The nature and extent of ballistic wounding is related to the energy transfer between bullet and tissue and the characteristics of the organs affected. Bullets cause injury by transferring their energy into the body tissues; the design of the bullet influences this process, with hollow nosed or dumdum bullets being designed to maximise energy transfer.

A high velocity bullet from a military rifle has more energy, and therefore greater wounding potential, than a handgun round. However, if it passes cleanly through a limb without striking bone, it may impart little of its energy to the victim and therefore cause a relatively minor wound.

Blast injury

Wounding may also be inflicted by explosive munitions such as rockets, aerial bombardment, mortars, and grenades. A small volume of explosive is converted to a large volume of gas in a very short time. This results in high pressure at the point of detonation, leading to the acceleration of gas molecules away from the explosion, a so called blast wind, the leading edge of which is the shock front.

Primary blast injury is typically experienced by casualties close to the explosion and is due to the interaction of this shock front on air-filled cavities within the body (middle ear, lung, bowel).

Secondary blast injury is due to impact on the body of items energised by the explosion. Modern munitions contain preformed metallic fragments; lacking aerodynamic features, such fragments rapidly lose velocity, resulting in low energy transfer pattern wounds.

Tertiary blast injury is seen when the victim is accelerated by the blast and thrown against a fixed object such as a wall.

Quaternary blast injury is that caused by collapse of any building secondary to a blast event.

Victims of blast often have multisystem injury, complicated by the presence of blunt and penetrating injury and burns.

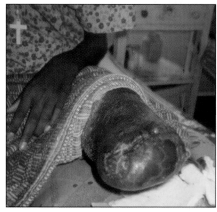

Healing amputation stump

Types of injury in modern warfare
- High energy transfer bullet wounds
- Fragmentation injury
- Blast injury
- Burns

Potential wounding energy of a missile:
$$\text{Kinetic energy} = \tfrac{1}{2}mv^2$$
Where m is the mass of the missile and v is its velocity

Cavitation secondary to high energy transfer bullet wound

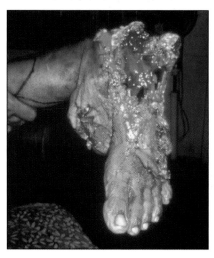

Lower limb disruption due to blast injury

Treating war injury

Initial measures

Initial measures for treating war injury are similar to those for any severe injury. Assessment and resuscitation of patients has traditionally been along the priorities of ABC—airway, breathing, and arrest of haemorrhage. Increasingly, however, prehospital military practice is to arrest haemorrhage first. This is because of the high incidence of death from exsanguination in war injured patients and the potential for simple first aid measures to prevent this.

Intravenous opiate analgesia and antibiotics should be given: the International Committee of the Red Cross (ICRC) recommends 5 MU (3000 mg) benzylpenicillin intravenously as soon as possible after wounding and continued 6 hourly for 24 hours. This is then changed to oral penicillin 500 mg 6 hourly (usually for a further four days). In the developing world patients might not have been immunised against tetanus. Grossly contaminated wounds containing devitalised tissue are at risk of infection with *Clostridium tetani*, and antitetanus serum and tetanus toxoid should be available.

Radiography, if available, is helpful in delineating fractures and detecting haemopneumothorax.

Wound assessment

After resuscitation, a careful top to toe survey must be done. Care must be taken to identify any truncal penetrating injury, without forgetting the back and buttocks, perineum, and axillae. Each wound must then be assessed and recorded. Wound assessment should include

- Site and size
- Presence of a cavity and degree of contamination
- Anatomical structures that may have been injured
- Distal perfusion
- Presence of fractures
- Whether a limb is so severely wounded as to be unreconstructable.

Wound excision

Wound excision involves removal of dead and contaminated tissue that, if left, would become a medium for infection. For limb wounds, a pneumatic tourniquet should be used if possible to reduce blood loss.

The first stage of the procedure is axial skin incision (debridement) in order to decompress the wound and allow post-traumatic swelling without constriction. These incisions should not cross joints longitudinally. Once decompression has been achieved, contamination should be removed and non-viable tissue excised. Skin is resilient, and only minimal excision is usually necessary, typically around the margin of the wound.

All foreign material should be removed from the wound, but obsessive pursuit of small metallic debris is not worth while. All dead and contaminated tissue should be excised, but determining the extent of the tissue that should be removed is often difficult. Dead muscle is dusky in colour, shows little tendency to bleed, and does not contract to forceps pressure.

Bone fragments denuded of soft tissue attachment should be removed; if left in the wound they will become infected and form osteomyelitic sequestrae. Injured nerves or tendons should be marked (with suture) for later repair.

At the end of the procedure the wound should be washed with copious quantities of saline and then left open. Apply a dry, bulky, sterile dressing.

Some low energy transfer wounds, such as those from most handguns, do not need extensive debridement and excision. These wounds can, in some circumstances, be managed without surgery.

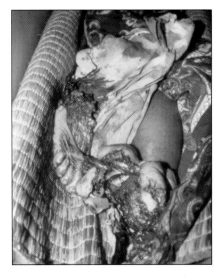

Acute landmine injury

Typical characteristics of war wounds

- Contaminated
- Contain devitalised tissue
- Affect more than one body cavity
- Often involve multiple injuries to the same patient
- 75% affect the limbs
- Often present late

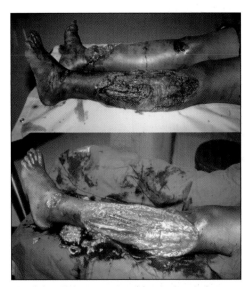

Blast injury before wound excision (top) and after wound excision (bottom)

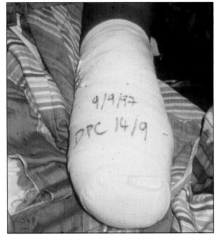

Wound left open with dry, bulky, sterile dressing

The optimal management of the multiple small fragment wounds often seen as a result of secondary blast injury is debated. The large number of these wounds precludes individual wound excision. There is no cavitation associated with such injury, and, because of the poor aerodynamic qualities of random fragments, the degree of penetration is usually not great. A reasonable approach is to clean all the wounds as thoroughly as possible by irrigation under general anaesthesia and then surgically debride only those major wounds associated with gross, deep contamination and tissue damage.

Delayed primary closure

Once wound excision has been done the patient can be returned to the ward for continued monitoring and analgesia. Dressings should be left in place and removed only when the patient returns to theatre for delayed primary closure. The ICRC recommends an interval of five days, but practice in the developed world now tends towards shorter periods of 48-72 hours. The only indication for return to theatre before this time has elapsed is signs of sepsis or an offensive smelling dressing. The commonest cause of sepsis is inadequate primary surgery.

The dressing should be removed in theatre with the patient under appropriate anaesthesia. If the wound shows no signs of infection, necrosis, or residual contamination it can be closed by suture or a split skin graft. However, multiple debridement may be required: in an ICRC series of amputations, only 45% were suitable for closure at first relook, with 33% of cases needing one further debridement and 22% needing two or more.

If closure is attempted, tension must be avoided. Rehabilitation can then start.

Amputation surgery

Some ballistic injuries, particularly those caused by landmines, will result in traumatic amputation of limbs. In others the limb injury is so severe that surgical amputation is necessary. The decision to amputate should come at the time of wound assessment. Scoring systems for limb injury are only poorly relevant to a ballistic pattern of injury. An insensate or avascular distal limb is a strong indication for amputation; seeking consensus with other surgical staff is helpful.

Skin and bone are relatively resistant to the propagation of blast and fragment, but muscle offers little impediment, and contamination can track along fascial planes. The extent of contamination and devitalisation of tissue is often more extensive than initially apparent.

Military surgeons have traditionally performed guillotine amputations, transecting skin, muscle, and bone all at the same level. Although this is quick and requires little surgical skill, it makes closure difficult, and the final amputation level is often more proximal than necessary. Most humanitarian surgical organisations recommend fashioning definitive flaps at initial surgery, maintaining stump length and facilitating early closure. The use of a myoplastic flap to cover the transected bone is strongly advocated.

Amputation should always be carried out under tourniquet to minimise blood loss. The surgical strategy is as for other war wounds; excise dead and contaminated tissue, determine the best functional level of amputation, and construct flaps to facilitate this. The wound should be left open and dressed with a dry, bulky, sterile dressing until delayed primary closure.

Competing interests: None declared.

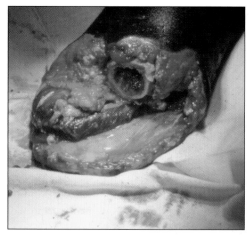
Clean wound, ready for delayed primary closure

Amputation surgery for war wounds

- Always under tourniquet
- Excise all dead and contaminated tissue
- Determine best functional level of amputation
- Fashion flaps using myoplastic technique
   For trans-tibial amputation, use medial gastrocnemius flap
   For trans-femoral amputation, use vastus lateralis or adductor magnus flap
- Leave wound open
- Delayed primary closure

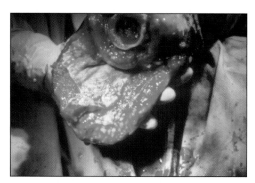
Primary myoplastic flap suitable for covering the transected bone of an amputation stump

---

Further reading

- Coupland RM. *War wounds of limbs.* Oxford: Butterworth-Heineman, 1993
- Molde A. *Surgery for victims of war.* 3rd ed. Geneva: ICRC Publications, 1998
- Roberts P. *The British military surgery pocket book.* British Army, 2004
- Mahoney PF, Ryan JM, Brooks A, Schwab CW, eds. *Ballistic trauma: a practical guide.* London: Springer Verlag, 2005
- King M, ed. *Primary surgery.* Vol 2. *Trauma.* Oxford: Oxford Medical Publications, 1993

7 The special needs of children and women

John Seaman, Sarah Maguire

The special needs of children

Children are more vulnerable to communicable diseases and environmental exposure than adults, have special dietary needs, and are generally dependent on their family for their material and emotional support.

Many of the most severe emergencies occur in poor countries. Poverty tends to exacerbate the impact of emergencies of all types: poor people live in low quality, damage-prone housing, often on marginal land at risk of landslide or flood. The children of the poor tend to have low nutritional status, increased exposure to communicable disease, low immunisation rates, high levels of intestinal parasites, and limited access to health care.

Queuing outside a clinic in Sudan

Earthquakes, floods, and other physical shocks
Trauma in these events may affect children disproportionally. In the 1976 Guatemala earthquake child mortality was generally higher than that of adults, but low in those less than 1 year old, attributed to the fact infants slept with their mother and were thus protected. Serious injury increased steadily with age, an effect assumed to result from the greater susceptibility to injury with increasing age.

In the 1971 Bangladesh cyclone children aged less than 10 years made up about a third of the population but accounted for half of all deaths. Many people survived this storm by clinging to trees. Mortality was particularly high in young children and in women older than 15 years, probably because of women trying to protect small children, the relative physical weakness of these groups, and the effects of exposure as the cyclone continued for many hours.

Economic consequences of disasters
The economic impact on families affected by disasters may be considerable. Houses, standing crops, domestic food stocks, livestock, and goods may be lost.

Crop failure and an increase in the price of food may lead to famine. The initial damage is often exacerbated by a fall in wages and the price of assets as many people attempt to find work and to sell livestock and other household goods to obtain food. In Malawi in 2001-2 an economic crisis was triggered by low food production because of flooding and the high price of fertilisers and other farm inputs and was aggravated by a reduction in national stocks. The poorest households had no food reserves and few assets, and, as the price of the staple maize increased almost fivefold, they could not obtain enough food.

The effects of economic shocks are typically three:
- Increased malnutrition rates due to a fall in the quantity and quality of food. Households may be reduced to consuming only cereals or roots, creating difficulties in feeding small children.
- Intensification of poverty. The loss of assets may reduce people to destitution. Even households that can survive may do so only by sacrificing expenditure on items such as education, soap, and clothing. Want may increase exposure to disease, such as HIV infection from increased prostitution.
- Population movement to roadsides and urban areas in search of food.

Risk assessment for humanitarian emergencies
- What health effects is the given shock likely to have on the population?
  Trauma, environmental exposure, disease transmission, and access to food and other necessities
- What were the conditions before the emergency?
  Adequacy of health services, immunisation coverage, nutritional status, etc
- What is the local capacity to respond to needs?
- How quickly will those needs arise and relief will be required?

Malnourished child and mother in a Nepalese clinic

Doctor assessment of untreated burns in a displaced people's camp

19

Population displacement to camps

Camps, whatever their origin, pose grave risks to life and health, particularly for children. High concentrations of people with low immunisation rates and high levels of pre-existing disease and without sanitation or adequate food supplies are optimal conditions for disease transmission through water, food, personal contact, and vectors. Most mortality in children results from measles, diarrhoeal and respiratory diseases, and malaria.

Camp populations often depend heavily on food aid, sometimes little more than cereal, and pellagra and scurvy have been known to become epidemic. The management of health and malnutrition is now largely standardised. Progress is tracked by monitoring mortality and anthropometric nutritional status.

War and conflict

Unicef estimated that, in 2001, 300 000 children younger than 18 years were acting as soldiers, guerrilla fighters, or in combat support roles in more than 50 countries around the world. Often, children are abducted from their families at very young ages (their parents may be killed), exposed to drugs, and forced to commit acts of barbarity.

At the end of a conflict, the children's greatest problems often relate to their fear of attack by community members when they go home. Girl mothers and their children are often stigmatised and neglected. Formerly abducted children often report that their greatest stress is not the residues of past violence but their inability to secure an economic livelihood. Many desperately desire education but have no resources or are too old to return to school.

Opinion is divided on the management of the psychological effects of emergencies on children. Some agencies argue for active intervention; others claim that this is therapeutically unproved and often impractical on any scale and that the best approach is to remove children from the brutality of war and restore them to social normality as quickly as possible, such as through family reunification when possible.

Special needs of women

It is essential to recognise the wider reality of women's lives if we are to establish and protect their human rights in emergency situations and if those providing aid in these crises are to meet their responsibilities.

Recognition

To understand how to respond to women, we need to find out what has been their experience of flight or persecution. Have they families or land left behind, have they had to grant sexual favours to cross borders or for humanitarian assistance? We need to ask questions and to pay attention to the answers, not to attach inappropriate cultural values to the answers or to deny their reality.

We need to explore the strategies women use to survive, bearing in mind that these may not always be to their own benefit (such as feeding everyone else in the family before themselves). Finally, we need to know what women can do; what is their untapped potential for coping and for providing longer term solutions to crises.

If women and girls feel that they have not been believed, they quickly learn that there is no point in telling painful and stigmatising stories. In many societies women are unwilling to speak if there are men present who can "say it better," or they are silent about their experiences for the sake of "moving on."

Similarly, women will often not insist on their ideas being heard. Humanitarian workers may struggle to create the space

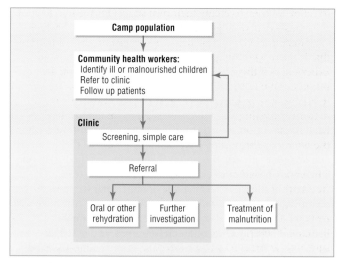

Organisation of food distribution in camps for displaced populations

Child art during the war in Sarajevo, indicating some of the psychological shocks that children experienced

Women preparing food in a displaced people's camp

"'Please listen to me; It would be good if you would listen to me' (girl soldier)"

From: Keairns YE. *The Voices of Girl Child Soldiers*. New York: Quaker United Nations Office, 2002

(or allow women to create their own space) for women to show solutions to the problems that they or their community face.

There is a belief, particularly in Western models of therapy, that it is wrong or dangerous to ask women about traumatic experiences if there is no time or space to follow it on. In humanitarian crises there is often no such time or space, yet not to ask because of these limitations may mean the difference between surviving and merely existing for many women. We have to ask ourselves whom we are really sparing if we don't ask the questions that elicit painful or difficult answers.

The rights based approach to women's experiences

International law is clear that just because people are victims of an emergency they do not lose their entitlement to dignity and respect. Women will often be the first to deny themselves in favour of others, particularly children or male partners, but any such discrimination in provision of services is contrary to international law and standards. The fact that women do cope, at least externally, means that, without a rights perspective, it is easy to relegate them to second place, be it for humanitarian assistance, appropriate health care, or provision of facilities.

Listening to women and adopting a rights perspective mean that humanitarian workers are less likely to impose their own understanding on a given situation. For example, girls and young women associated with demobilising soldiers may be assumed to be legitimate family members or "camp followers" and may thus be deprived of any independent benefits when appearing at demobilisation facilities and assumed to be content to go with their "husband" to his home, even if they were abducted from somewhere completely different.

Violence against women is so much a part of modern conflicts and other crises, and women are so silent about it and silenced by it, that it is easy to lose a sense of outrage and to forget that this is a gross human rights violation.

Responsibilities of workers involved in humanitarian crises

Workers have a responsibility not to exacerbate problems and not to participate (directly or indirectly) in ill treatment, but they also have a responsibility to ensure that women are treated with full human rights. It can be difficult to be the lone voice for women's rights when there is peer pressure to be passive in the name of neutrality or confidentiality.

When non-governmental organisations learn of acts of physical violence they often have to decide how to record that information so that the twin objectives of providing information for justice and maintaining their neutrality (so they can work in similar places in the future) are both met. It is not a matter of compromising one objective for the other, but of finding ways to pursue both.

Responsible treatment also means keeping abreast of the relevant law. It was only in 2002 that the International Criminal Tribunal in The Hague defined sexual offences as a crime against humanity. Similarly, it is only relatively recently that sexual violence in refugee camps has been identified by relief agencies as an issue that needs formal attention and response.

Conclusions

Humanitarian workers must make special efforts to understand what women have experienced and what contribution they can make to finding solutions to the crisis and must treat women with dignity and respect. This means providing assistance without discrimination, which in turn means paying attention to women's particular needs and situations. The responsibility of medical staff to provide appropriate treatment does not end as the woman leaves the tent or clinic but continues into accurate and impartial recording.

"Both the experience of conflict itself and the impact of conflict on access to health care determine the physical health and the psychological well being of women and girls in very particular ways. Women are not only victims of the general violence and lack of health care—they also face issues specific to their biology and social status. They add to the complexity of the picture, women also carry the burden of caring for others, including those who are sick, injured, elderly or traumatised. This in itself is stressful and often contributes to illness"

From: Rehn E, Johnson-Sirleaf E. *Women, war, peace: The independent experts' assessment.* New York: Unifem, 2002

Treatment of women affected by humanitarian crises*

- Psychosocial support and reproductive health services for women to be an integral part of emergency assistance and reconstruction
  Special attention should be paid to those who experienced physical trauma, torture, and sexual violence
  All agencies providing health support and social services should include psychosocial counselling and referrals
- Recognition of the special health needs of women who have experienced war related injuries, including amputations, and equal provision of physical rehabilitation and prosthesis support
- Special attention to providing adequate food supplies for displaced women, girls, and families to protect health and to prevent the sexual exploitation of women and girls
- United Nations, donors, and governments to provide long term financial support for women survivors of violence through legal, economic, psychosocial, and reproductive health services
  This should be an essential part of emergency assistance and reconstruction
- Protection against HIV/AIDS and provision of reproductive health through implementation of the minimum initial services package as defined in *Reproductive Health in Refugee Situations: An Inter-agency Field Manual* (WHO, UNHCR, UFPA, 1999)
  Special attention must be paid to the needs of particularly vulnerable groups such as displaced women, adolescents, girl headed households, and sex workers
- Immediate provision of emergency contraception and treatment for sexually transmitted diseases for rape survivors to prevent unwanted pregnancies and protect the health of women

*Adapted from: Rehn E, Johnson-Sirleaf E. *Women, war, peace: The independent experts' assessment.* New York: Unifem, 2002. Though written for conflict settings, the recommendations are equally applicable to other humanitarian crises

---

Further reading

- Sphere Project. *Humanitarian charter and minimum standards in disaster response.* Geneva: Sphere Project, 2004 www.sphereproject.org
- Bracken PJ, Petty C. *Rethinking the trauma of war.* London: Free Association Books, 1998
- UNICEF (United Nations Children's Fund) www.unicef.org
- Macrae J, Zwi A. *War and hunger: rethinking international response to complex emergencies.* London: Zed Books and Save the Children, 1994
- Sphere Project. *Humanitarian charter and minimum standards in disaster response.* Geneva: Sphere Project, 2004. www.sphereproject.org
- Marie Stopes International. www.mariestopes.org.uk
- United Nations High Commissioner for Refugees. *Reproductive health in refugee situations—an inter-agency field manual.* Geneva: UNHCR, 1999
- Bracken PJ, Petty C. *Rethinking the trauma of war.* London: Free Association Books, 1998

Competing interests: None declared.

8   Displaced populations and long term humanitarian assistance

Maria Kett

Conflicts and disasters—whether manufactured or natural—often result in the wide scale displacement of people. This may be as a result of destruction of homes and environment, religious or political persecution, or simply economic necessity. Some remain internally displaced within the borders of their own country, if not their own region or homeland. Others will cross international borders as refugees. (A refugee is legally defined as someone who has crossed an international border to escape actual or potential persecution.)

Whatever the reason for displacement, the resulting mass of vulnerable people, most of whom may be women and children, must be accommodated somewhere, be it in tented camps, semipermanent or permanent collective centres or settlements, or even private residences.

For healthcare professionals contributing to humanitarian missions and projects in the acute phase of population displacement, an awareness of some of the factors that can influence the long term outcomes can be of great benefit for understanding project implications and sustainability.

Issues in humanitarian responses

Humanitarian responses can be considered under the phases of early or emergency, post-emergency or intermediate, and resettlement or long term (these phases overlap and are not necessarily sequential). This article focuses on continued responses in the long term resettlement phase.

Responsibilities

While the United Nations High Commission for Refugees (UNHCR) is legally bound by international statute to assist and protect refugees, this is not so for internally displaced people—though the commission often does take responsibility for them, as set out in its *Guiding Principles on Internal Displacement*.

Other agencies that share responsibility for refugees and internally displaced people include the International Committee of the Red Cross (although its mandate ceases when conflict ends), the UN children's fund Unicef, and many smaller non-governmental organisations with varying specialties.

Responsibilities change with time, and the duty of care to internally displaced people in settlements and camps often will, and should, eventually shift back to the host government. However, several closely related factors affect this decision.

Duration of displacement

Displacement may be for a considerable time, which raises questions about living conditions, the possibility of resettlement, the availability of land and houses, and ongoing security issues, including fear of persecution and physical and psychological trauma experienced during conflict. It also brings into question the role of governments, international agencies, and non-governmental organisations in these processes.

Resolution of displacement

A host of factors affect resolution of displacement.
● Political—Will of the international community or host government; political influence of the displaced group; issues of responsibility for the displaced people

Camp for refugees and internally displaced people

Potential causes of displacement

Natural disasters	Human made events
● Floods	● War
● Earthquakes	● Political upheaval or revolution
● Tsunamis	● Religious or political persecution
● Volcanoes	● Development projects (such as
● Tropical storms	hydroelectric dams)
● Famine	● Chemical or toxic spills
● Landslides	● Nuclear incidents

Changes in humanitarian response and responsibility over time

Early or emergency phase	→	Resettlement or long term phase
Type of response		
Emergency relief	→	Sustainable development
Responsibility		
Aid agencies (Need exit strategy)	→	Host government (Needs appropriate political and economic conditions)

Statistics for internally displaced people

Country	No of people and length of time that they have been displaced
Afghanistan	600 000 for ≥ 20 years
Angola	1.4 million for ≥ 27 years
Azerbaijan	1 million for ≥ 8 years
Bosnia	1 million for ≥ 8 years
Burundi	281 000 for ≥ 20 years
Liberia	600 000 for ≥ 14 years
Palestinian Territories	250 000 for ≥ 20 years
Sudan	4.3 million for ≥ 20 years

Data from Global IDP Project. Internal displacement: a global overview of trends and developments in 2003. www.idpproject.org/global_overview.htm

Worldwide, internally displaced people now outnumber conventional refugees by 2:1

- External funding—Influenced by the political factors above; the strategic importance of the affected region; and media interest in the crisis
- Resources in affected region—State of the economy; level of infrastructure and housing; level of economic growth or poverty
- Friction—Attitude of indigent population to incomers; protracted conflict; ethnic or nationalist tensions
- Role of aid agencies—Risk of creating "aid dependency" and a society functioning on handouts that loses the ability to manage and care for itself; conditions for sustainable development or regeneration.

Human security issues of displacement

The UN Development Programme (UNDP) in 1994 highlighted seven human security indicators, which act as a useful benchmark for the long term provision of care to displaced people.

Economic security (assured basic income)
Many aspects of this are beyond health workers' jurisdiction as it is related to overall infrastructure development. But remember that good general health, including rehabilitation from conflict related injuries, enables people to seek employment.

Food security (physical and economic access to food)
After the initial emergency phase of displacement, which incorporates therapeutic feeding programmes and provision of food supplies, a health worker's role may shift from the more practical to the dispensing of nutritional advice.

Health security (relative freedom from disease and infection)
Swift resumption of primary care services after a crisis can be more beneficial for the health of the affected population than intensive emergency medical and surgical aid. This means integrating displaced people into local healthcare structures and informing them about the care provided.

Health issues will inevitably shift in emphasis from acute problems to chronic conditions and from curative to preventive medicine. This raises questions about funding and provision, and whether treatments are available, accessible, sustainable, and affordable. Caution is necessary when starting a treatment (from simple dressings to drugs or psychosocial work) that may be difficult to continue once a non-governmental organisation has ceased to provide aid.

Health workers should be particularly aware of long term problems among the most vulnerable populations—elderly or disabled people, women, and children.

Environmental security (access to clean water and air and non-degraded land)
Environmental issues, such as a functioning sewerage system, electricity, running water, and refuse collection have an obvious impact on living standards and health. Such services are often unavailable or severely disrupted immediately after a disaster or conflict and may not be a priority in terms of long term infrastructure repair.

They may also not be seen as a priority by the displaced population if it is given responsibility to organise and pay for these public utilities, as happened in Bosnia. After eight years of providing subsidised utilities, the municipalities decided to charge the beneficiaries. Unaccustomed to paying bills, the beneficiaries in one camp let the debt accumulate until their electricity supply was finally cut off.

Internally displaced people living long term in abandoned railway carriages

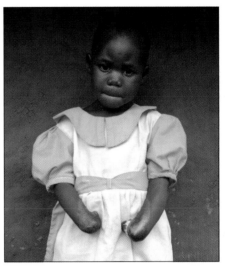
Long term management of conflict related injuries, such as these deliberate amputations, can allow displaced people to seek employment

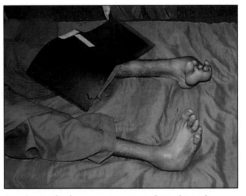
As a humanitarian response moves from the early phase, health care will shift in emphasis from managing acute problems to treating chronic disabilities and conditions

---

Common long term medical problems in internally displaced communities

Bosnia	Azerbaijan
• Type 2 diabetes	• Minor gynaecological disorders
• Hypertension	• Groin hernia
• Coronary artery disease	• Tonsillectomy
• Stress related illnesses	• Thyroid disease
• Gynaecological complaints	• Burns and skin grafting
• Asthma	

Personal security (security from violence and threats)

The threat of land mines, unexploded ordnance, and gunfire affect both personal and environmental security and pose a considerable challenge to regeneration after conflict. Both internally displaced people and returnees face fear and intimidation from opposing political or ethnic groups in many post-conflict zones. Women and children in particular face harassment and danger in camps and centres, not only from opposition groups but also from members of their own communities.

Community security (security of cultural identity)

Loss of a homeland can lead to a loss of cultural identity. Cultural and ethnic groups may be dispersed and segregated after displacement. Security, dignity, and freedom to be educated and to practise cultural and religious beliefs are essential to preserving a sense of identity. Religious or community leaders often act as spokespeople in camps, and so an understanding of sensitive cultural issues is vital. Health care may also offer a neutral ground for reconciliation between communities.

Political security (protection of basic human rights)

Internally displaced people have the right to be treated with the same respect and dignity afforded to all citizens of their country. These rights continue if and when displaced people return home.

Resolving displacement

There are three possible resolutions to displacement: return and repatriation, resettlement, or asylum in another country. Each option has its own problems and requires a great deal of support.

The decision to end internal displacement should be voluntary, and depend on legislative, political, economic, and social reforms and the successful transition to peace or a return to "normality." The return process can be difficult to monitor and assess, however, as it is usually the responsibility of the host country. Displaced people should not feel forced to return, but the issues that mitigate against a return are often the same as those against remaining. These include infrastructure, security, employment, land, health care, and housing.

Many humanitarian projects cease when displaced people return home, but many returnees continue to need support, particularly in areas such as health care and education, for which the infrastructure is often still in the early phase of regeneration.

Conclusion

In a humanitarian response, aid agencies must consider their long term goals. Over an extended period, some internally displaced populations can and do adapt to their circumstances, creating their own conditions for coping, and even becoming self sufficient. However, many others become increasingly vulnerable and socially excluded.

The end of displacement is invariably a gradual process, requiring continued and sustainable support. This is particularly important for health care. Health professionals work in tandem with many other agencies and specialists in the field and have a vital role in the continuing care, assessment, and treatment of long term displaced populations.

The photograph of a Ugandan girl with amputated hands was taken by Chris Steele-Perkins and supplied by Magnum Photos.

In Bosnia, as in many places round the world, new generations of internally displaced people are growing up never having known a homeland or a settled way of life

Azerbaijan resettlement camp, one of the possible ways of ending displacement

Further reading

- Global IDP Project. Internal displacement: a global overview of trends and developments in 2003. www.idpproject.org/global_overview.htm
- Weiss Fagen P. Looking beyond emergency response. *Forced Migration Review* 2003;17:19-21
- The Sphere Project. Humanitarian charter and minimum standards in disaster response. www.sphereproject.org/
- Ryan J, Mahoney PF, Greaves I, Bowyer G, eds. *Conflict and catastrophe medicine—a practical guide.* London: Springer-Verlag, 2002
- Médecins Sans Frontières. *Refugee health—an approach to emergency situations.* London: Macmillan, 1997
- International Committee of the Red Cross. www.icrc.org/
- UNHCR: the UN refugee agency. www.unhcr.ch/
- Levy BS, Sidel VW. *War and public health.* Oxford: Oxford University Press, 1997

Competing interests: None declared.

9 Psychological aspects of providing medical humanitarian aid

Ian Palmer

All those involved in either a catastrophe or conflict will be changed by the experience. Such change, however small, is irreversible but generally positive. Only a minority of survivors or aid workers will develop a mental disorder such as post-traumatic stress disorder. Humanitarian deployments may be isolating, rife with personal threat (from climate, endemic diseases, violence), and expose individuals to human misery, as well as human resourcefulness in the face of tragedy.

You should deploy only if you are in good physical and mental health. Accept that everyone in your family will be changed by your deployment and that any problems you leave behind will be there on your return: sort them out before you go. Discuss potential outcomes with your family (such as death or being taken hostage) and make a will.

Proper planning and preparation prevent poor performance. Preparation requires information: get as much as you can. The best sources are people who have been to the disaster area before. Beware of media selectivity and bias, and protect family and friends from this after deployment through regular communication.

Children left homeless and traumatised by the 2004 tsunami, Nagapattinam, Tamil Nadu, India. Misery and grief are inevitable consequences of catastrophes, and no one who encounters them will remain unchanged

Expatriate work stressors

Remember you are a "guest" in the country and are there to help local people to help themselves, not to create dependency. Treat all with dignity, especially the dead, who may have died without it. Aim to foster cooperation and the restoration of motivation, self belief, and self sufficiency.

Humanitarian disasters are confusing, and teamwork is vital; leadership means leading by example, and praise and interest are key. Protocols, if understood and followed, are useful, but flexibility is crucial. Some colleagues may have personalities that make them difficult to get on with, or they may develop frank mental illness or drink or drug related problems.

Be aware of what internal pressures you create and can alter and accept those external pressures that you cannot change. Beware of malicious gossip; it is endemic in expatriate communities and corrosive to group functioning. The temptation to relieve stress through alcohol, drugs, and sex should be tempered with knowledge of their potential pitfalls.

It is natural to feel homesick and "down" at times, and support may be drawn from religious faith, belief in mission, communications with family and friends, home comforts, and letters and parcels.

Community responses to disaster

Immediate—Initially survivors are devastated and emotionally labile. Panic is uncommon unless escape is felt to be impossible, and then it is contagious. External help is required to clean up and rebuild. Somatic symptoms are common.

Short to medium term—Excessive dependency is common in the first 48 hours, after which there is a period of searching for meaning in what has happened. This may be followed by hostility: aid workers may become a focus of resentment, on whom feelings of frustration, betrayal, and anger can be projected. Group loyalties or contradictory roles can greatly affect individual and group behaviours. Survivors of massive

---

Vital pre-deployment questions for humanitarian workers:
  Why am I going?
  Who am I going with?
  Are my expectations realistic?

Risk factors associated with popular ways to relieve stress

Alcohol
- Aggression
- Risk taking
- Drunk driving (you, colleagues, and local drivers)
- Sexual (mis)adventures, with the attendant risks of venereal diseases
- If alcohol is used to deal with stress, insomnia will in time only confound the original problem

Drugs
- Effects may be unpredictable
- May precipitate acute psychotic mental illness
- Risk of HIV infection with injected drugs

Sexual liaisons
- Take contraceptives with you—and use them (that's the hard part)

Psychological reactions to disaster or catastrophe

- About 25% of people remain effective, with emotional continence and appropriate behaviours
- Some 50-75% are "normal" but bewildered, "numb," withdrawn, and anxious
- About 15% are ineffective from the outset, with inappropriate "contagious" behaviours

disaster may develop a "concentration camp mentality," in which they become selfish, compassionless, and focused on personal survival.

Long term—Normality returns gradually with reconstruction and rebuilding through acknowledgement, acceptance, and accommodation to change.

Psychological effects of conflict and disaster

Do not impose your own beliefs on others or try to understand how local populations view loss and illness. Distress and change are the inevitable results of exposure to unpleasant events; mental disorder is not.

Exposure to extreme stress does not seem to increase the incidence of psychoses, and even neurotic mental disorders are uncommon. Post-traumatic mental disorders include depression, anxiety, post-traumatic stress disorder, phobias, medically unexplained symptoms, substance misuse, and personality change.

Any psychological reaction or disorder is multifactorial in genesis and depends on a unique interaction between the individual, the event, the psychosocial environment, and the culture from which the individual comes and to which he or she returns.

Azeri adolescent's painting of an injured child

Prevention and management

As prevention is better than cure, most early interventions should be social in nature—freedom from threat of death, and access to shelter, clean water, food, and sanitation.

Efforts should be directed at reuniting families and societies and returning them to normality—for example, schooling for children and the dignity of work for adults. Every effort should be made to address culturally relevant interventions, rituals, and spiritual needs. It may, for example, be of more psychological benefit to survivors of war crimes to see their tormentors brought to justice than to be offered psychological debriefing. Although specific psychiatric interventions have a role, care must be taken to avoid their misplaced use ("cultural imperialism").

Without exposure to traumatic events, post-traumatic stress disorder cannot occur; it is therefore important to avoid potential hazards such as sites of atrocities. Protect the security and safety of those with whom you work by sticking to prescribed routes and ensuring you know, and make known, where you and others are going and when you are returning.

Time and social integrity are important in any healing process. Never start things that cannot be finished, especially in the area of psychosocial responses to catastrophe and disaster.

Former Bosnian Serb internal affairs minister and national police chief Mico Stanisic facing charges of crimes against humanity. Seeing the perpretrators brought to justice may be of more psychological benefit to survivors of war crimes than being offered counselling

Specific psychiatric situations

Treating mental illness is seldom a priority in countries ravaged by disaster or war. There is no evidence that the incidence of psychotic illness increases after such events; indeed, mental illness may diminish during community upheaval, as people "come together" to help each other. That there is a psychological cost cannot be doubted, but it may be a Western conceit to medicalise such misery and distress.

Efforts can be made to restore mental hospitals, communities, or institutions, but they will rarely be seen as a priority. Psychotic patients have the same basic needs as everyone else—safety and shelter, clean water, and food. Drugs will be needed, and agencies such as Pharmaciens Sans Frontières can help.

The psychological cost of conflict and disaster is obvious, but it may be a Western conceit to medicalise such distress

Specific psychosocial issues

Interpersonal violence–Justice is a potent psychological intervention. As a humanitarian worker, you can help by collecting any evidence you can of acts against human rights, particularly rape and torture. In such cases certain psychological interventions may be useful but must be handled in a culturally sensitive way to avoid further "injury." Never medicalise people; treat them with respect as survivors. Do not expect them to trust you, and never persuade them to tell you their story unless it (and you) are part of a therapeutic programme. Humanitarian workers may be taken hostage and abused; ensure that your aid agency tells you what support you may receive if this happens.

Disabled people–People disabled by catastrophe or war are in special need extending over the long term. Great effort, sensitivity, and tact are required to restore shattered bodies to the dignity of economic independence.

Soldiers–Both child soldiers and demobilised soldiers have specific needs that are best addressed socially, but the groups reintroducing them into peaceful life and work may need to provide psychological advice to help with rehabilitation.

Repatriation

Repatriation is about readjusting to your previous life and to the changes that have occurred in yourself and in your family. In general, the more problematic the deployment the more problematic the readjustment. Your expectations of reunion will not be met if they are unrealistic or if you have not prepared yourself realistically.

Problems on return?

Generally, traumatic events will upset you when you think about them or images intrude on your thoughts. This may lead to avoidance, which is potentially damaging. You may also become irritable and irascible, which will create interpersonal difficulties. It is important to find someone (safe for you) who can listen to you; in this way most problems resolve with the passage of time.

You should, however, seek further help if you feel that you want help, if someone you respect or care about suggests that you have "changed," or if you have symptoms of a stress related problem that are severe or are not settling after 6-12 weeks and are interfering with your life. Suitable sources of help are:

- Those who shared the experience
- Family and friends
- Through your aid agency, which should have access to or be able to direct you to psychological support
- Through your family doctor
- Psychiatric and psychological professionals
- A traumatic stress service such as that run by University College Hospital, London, and Maudsley Hospital, London
- If you have been tortured, the Medical Council for the Victims of Torture.

The photograph of Indian children left homeless by the 2004 tsunami was supplied by Chris Stowers/Panos Pictures. The photograph of Mico Stanisic was supplied by AP Photo/Fred Ernst.

Competing interests: None declared.

Rwandan children's drawings of the impact of war on their family and of witnessed events

Preparation for repatriation

Review
- Review the deployment as a group
- How has the experience changed you?
- How will the experience benefit you?
- What you would do differently next time?
- What would you tell other people going to the same area? Write a report and keep a copy

Evaluate expectations
- Yours, your family's, and friends'
- What to do if you feel no one understands
- How will you deal with routine work?

Managing questions
- Routinely:
  What will you say when people ask about your experiences?
  What will you do when they stop asking?
  What questions will you ask?
- After gruesome experiences:
  What will you tell people without distressing them?

Symptoms of a stress related problem

- Intrusive thoughts, images, or smells triggered by people, places, media reports, etc
- Avoiding such "triggers"
- Avoiding friends and social situations—becoming socially withdrawn
- Relationship problems, especially if related to irritability and anger
- Disturbed sleep, poor concentration
- Becoming overanxious, depressed, or miserable
- Drinking too much, misusing drugs
- Acting "out of character" and impulsively

Further reading

- Bracken PJ, Petty C, eds. *Rethinking the trauma of war.* London: Free Association Books, 1988
- UN High Commission for Refugees. *Guidelines on the evaluation and care of victims of trauma and violence.* Geneva: UNHCR, 1993
- Summerfield D. The impact of war and atrocity on civilian populations. In: Black D, Newman M, Harris-Hendriks J, Mezey G. *Psychological trauma: a developmental approach.* London: Gaskell, 1997
- Basoglu M, ed. *Torture and its consequences: current treatment approaches.* Cambridge: Cambridge University Press, 1992
- Palmer IP. Psychosocial costs of war in Rwanda. *Advances in Psychiatric Treatment* 2002;8:17-25

10 Conflict recovery and intervening in hospitals

James M Ryan, Peter F Mahoney, Cara Macnab

Conflict recovery

The essence of conflict is the actual or implied use of violence. Recovery implies a return to a previous state. Recovery may be rapid (measured in months) or may take many years. The timing of recovery varies: it may start during the acute phase of a crisis (provision of humanitarian assistance in the midst of conflict can be the earliest manifestation of recovery) but usually begins in the post-emergency phase, when a degree of stability and safety allows a more comprehensive approach.

Time line and phases

Recovery from disaster or conflict can be considered as having a series of phases—emergency response and transition, early recovery, medium term recovery, and long term development.

Emergency response and transition—The emergency humanitarian response in the crisis phase is the aspect of humanitarian work most widely observed by the media and best understood by the general public. Aid agencies deploy and work in the full glare of publicity. This phase passes, and a transitional phase begins, often characterised by the departure of many of the immediate response agencies and the media. The tragedy slips from public consciousness.

Early recovery—This phase starts with the ending of hostilities. It is a period of relative safety, but money, staff, and equipment often become scarce—despite earlier promises of aid, the tap is turned down, if not off. There then starts a period of uncertainty, which is open ended, difficult, and unglamorous.

Medium term recovery—By now, the affected region should have some form of government, even if this is externally imposed. The process of rebuilding infrastructure has begun, and recognisable instruments of a functioning state become evident, such as health and education ministries, the emergence of a civil service, and police. This period requires specialised aid.

Long term development—Long term recovery should have as its end point not just a return to the pre-conflict state but a state where the accepted instruments of good governance are in place and the region is capable of independent existence. The process may take decades, and in some cases the target is never reached. This is typically the case in so called failed states.

Intervention in hospitals

Non-governmental organisations and intergovernmental organisations generally work effectively in basic health care. Money spent here has a greater impact on the population as a whole than money spent on hospitals. Restoring a water supply and providing food and a sanitation system are more important, technically easier, and cheaper than restoring and maintaining a failed general hospital in a conflict setting.

Hospitals, irrespective of their location, are notoriously expensive to run with heavy consumption of scarce resources. They are complex organisations requiring a long term multi-agency commitment and can fail again if support is withdrawn prematurely. There is little evidence that restoring hospital services improves population survival immediately after a conflict or disaster. There is, however, a price to pay in the medium and longer term if hospitals are not assisted.

Levels of healthcare intervention after conflict or disaster

Emergency needs

Basic curative care needs of residents of emergency settlements are typically

- Treatment of diarrhoea
- Treatment of acute respiratory infections
- Treatment of other prevalent conditions (such as malaria)
- Therapeutic feeding
- Care of wounds
- Psychological counselling or the equivalent

During recovery phases

Basic model for organising health service systems is three tiered:

Primary care

- Clinics for children <5 years old, routine immunisation, rehydration centres, malaria screening and treatment, diagnosis and treatment of pneumonia, outreach programmes, antenatal and delivery care
- Training and supervision of community health workers, traditional birth attendants, and traditional healers, who can play an important role, especially for collective health awareness and notification of cases during epidemic outbreaks

Secondary care

- Inpatient services for severe cases requiring triage and surveillance—such as treatment for complications of childbirth

Tertiary care

- System of referral to hospitals for surgery and severely ill patients, and access to laboratory facilities for diagnosis and disease confirmation
- Arrangement and payment for transportation and other logistical details must be agreed in advance by administrators of the emergency settlement community health programme and the hospital administration, usually through the ministry of health

Adapted by Eric K Noji from: University of Wisconsin Disaster Management Center: *First international emergency settlement conference: new approaches to new realities. April 15-19, 1996.* Madison WI: University of Wisconsin Disaster Management Center, 1996

Empty shelves in the pharmacy of a failed hospital in Afghanistan

It is also important to understand the degree to which a hospital has failed; hospitals in post-conflict areas may be

- Functioning—retaining most or all of their pre-conflict capability and capacity
- Compromised—having lost some capability or capacity
- Failed—having no residual capability or capacity.

Intervention priorities

Hospital needs assessment requires expert involvement if aid interventions and use of scarce resources are to be effective, and inappropriate equipment donations and projects avoided.

Security—No assistance is possible if dangers have not been addressed. This may entail the exclusion of armed gangs and militias from hospital buildings and making safe unexploded ordnance. Staff and patients may need physical protection.

Repair of infrastructure—Electrical power for lighting and heating or air conditioning; water supply; food provision, storage, and preparation; and sanitation are immediate needs.

Clinical and professional staffing—Key staff may be found locally and supplemented by aid agency health workers, at least for a time. There are financial issues; in a failed state the assisting agency may have to pay local staff a small stipend, at least enough for food and life's essentials for staff and their families. Negotiated collaboration between agency and local staff may be necessary and requires diplomatic handling.

Management and administrative structure—This may still survive, at least partially, or be non-existent. If aid agency staff take over, careful liaison is needed to avoid conflict.

Agreement on immediate clinical priorities—This can only be considered when all of the above have been accomplished. This will be a multi-agency task. As a rule, salvage of life and limb will be the priority.

Hospital equipment and supplies—These will be determined by agreeing immediate clinical priorities. Occasionally, however, the situation may be reversed, with clinical priorities being determined by the availability of scarce resources.

Parallel systems

In the new climate of humanitarian assistance, particularly in the context of intrastate conflict and failed states, a climate of danger may be present. This has resulted in the increasing involvement of military medical personnel in providing humanitarian assistance, including hospital care.

It is not unusual for military and non-governmental organisation emergency hospitals to be established in close proximity. Both may become involved in local hospital interventions, not always in harmony. There is an urgent need to establish "rules of engagement" for such eventualities. When collaborating and communicating well, these parallel ventures can yield enormous benefit.

Difficult decisions—long term hospital planning

Some hospitals will simply not survive the collapse of a state, and new solutions may be needed such as early closure decisions and a reorganisation of surviving institutions. This may require changes of site and relocation or require major structural rebuilding on original sites. Hospitals deemed unlikely to survive alone may retain their history and institutional memory while merging with more viable institutions. These decisions should be made by local officials and not be imposed by external agencies.

Case Study 1: Caucasus—Baku, Azerbaijan

The situation in Azerbaijan in 1997 can be summarised as

- 70 years of Soviet control
- Territorial war with Armenia and the former Soviet Union
- 20% loss of national territory

Why do hospitals fail?

- Loss of physical infrastructure—deliberate or accidental targeting of buildings by warring factions
- Loss of utilities—especially power, water, food supply, and sanitation
- Loss of skilled staff—attacked, stopped from working, or from across ethnic divide
- Failure of routine services with loss of planned procedures, chronic care, cancer care, complex surgery, and supporting services; followed by loss of emergency and urgent care
- Loss of emergency medical services and referral system, so patients cannot reach those facilities still functioning
- Loss of consumables, drugs, and related items
- Breakdown in morale and motivation—often associated with loss of pay and inability to provide essential services
- Forced closure, with or without ejection of staff by combatants—often associated with civil strife and "ethnic cleansing"

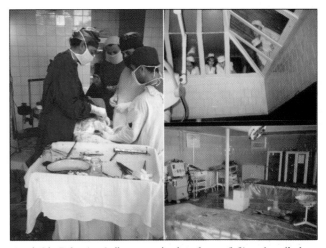

Hospital in Baku, Azerbaijan: operating in a theatre (left), and medical students preparing to view surgery (right)

Viewing x rays in a theatre in a Baku hospital

Common features in Baku hospitals

- Dereliction of hospital buildings
- Breakdown of hospital facilities
- Collapse of diagnostic and clinical support facilities
- Departure of senior professional staff
- Loss of morale and low self esteem among remaining medical staff
- Loss of local, national, and international professional networks, leading to professional and academic isolation
- Collapse of research and development programmes
- Loss of salary and reward, leading to institutional corruption
- Disruption of day to day medical care of patients

- Destruction of industrial, agricultural, and medico-social infrastructure
- One million refugees and internally displaced people
- Breakdown of the national health system.

Hospitals in the capital city, Baku, were geographically distant from the zone of conflict, but they felt the consequences of the collapse of the economy and social and medical infrastructure. In each hospital certain features were common.

Some hospitals fared better than others. Those that managed to remain functioning tended to have better staffing and some income from private practice or support from international aid agencies. Much depended on the efforts of individuals. In the Academic Trauma Institute, one consultant orthopaedic surgeon made his own instruments and external fixators in his small engineering workshop.

A consequence of the failure of central health care was that refugees and displaced people in camps throughout Azerbaijan were virtually cut off from any form of hospital care.

Azerbaijan is now a recovering nation with the prospect of oil and natural gas revenues to fund the restoration of its infrastructure. Pre-hospital and primary care is improving. Despite this, the country is still some way from entering a recognisable development phase. This impasse is due, in the main, to the unresolved territorial dispute with Armenia, resulting in the continuing presence of nearly one million displaced people in camps cared for by international aid agencies.

Case study 2: Balkans—Pristina, Kosovo

In the summer of 1999 Kosovo was in a well defined acute emergency phase with an expected rapid transition to early recovery phase. The territory had experienced civil war, population displacement, and NATO intervention. The returning population, displaced internally and to neighbouring countries, faced damaged and destroyed housing, a collapsed infrastructure, and no instruments of government. In such a vacuum, the United Nations interim administration became the government, with the World Food Programme feeding the population and the World Health Organization taking on the health portfolio. The World Bank took control of finance.

There was an immediate need to create the essentials of a new health system out of the surviving remnants of the centralised model that had existed before 1999. Agencies involved included NATO, United Nations, Department for International Development, and many non-governmental organisations. The position with regard to the territory's only teaching hospital, the 2400 bed University Hospital Pristina, shows the difficulties encountered when taking over a major general and specialist teaching hospital.

The emergency phase initially attracted considerable media interest, but this soon waned. With this passing interest, resources and international expertise dwindled. The initial optimism of a rapid move to early and medium term recovery, and later a development phase, was replaced by what one aid agency colleague termed the "long haul syndrome."

Summary

Practical and meaningful interventions during the recovery from a conflict or disaster are diffuse, complex, and open ended. The problems outlined in this article for hospitals might as easily be applied to restoration of other services (such as education systems), assistance to industry or agriculture, and restoration of vital government departments.

Competing interests: None declared.

Ward kitchen sink in a Baku children's hospital

Intervention in Pristina Hospital

- Securing and demilitarising the hospital and related facilities
  Included removing barricades, booby traps, and anti-personnel mines
- Restoration of electricity, water, and food supplies and sanitation
  Included provision of generators and water pumps and removal of a large collection of discarded clinical waste
  Also included clearing the mortuary, which had failed refrigerators and was overflowing, with bodies lying in corridors and passageways
- Organisation of remaining staff and facilities. Problems included
  Most pre-existing staff (mainly Serbs) had fled
  Most incoming staff (Albanian) had no proof of identity or training, having been sacked by the Serbian government in 1991
  Hospital records and important documentation had been destroyed
  Clinical case notes had been destroyed
  Clinical support facilities (imaging, laboratory, pharmacy, and intensive care unit) not functioning
  Complete absence of a management structure
  Complete breakdown of clinical teaching and medical education
- Establishment of a hospital management and administrative system
  To avoid conflict, non-native aid workers were initially appointed to key positions
- Establishment of a medical provision and supply system
- Establishment of a postgraduate medical education programme

Further reading

- Fleggson M. Fast track to recovery. *Health Exchange* 2003;Feb:8-10
- Hayward-Karlsson J. *Hospitals for war-wounded.* Geneva: ICRC, 1998
- Ignatieff M. *The warrior's honor: ethnic war and the modern conscience.* New York: Henry Holt, 1998
- Kegley CW, Wittkopf ER. *World politics: trends and transformation.* London: Macmillan, 1999
- Médicins Sans Frontières. *Refugee health: an approach to emergency situations.* London: Macmillan, 1997
- Perrin P. *War and public health.* Geneva: ICRC, 1996
- Redmond T. How do you eat an elephant? *BMJ* 1999;319:1652-3
- Ryan JM. The neglected challenge of war and conflict. *Health Exchange* 2002;Feb:5-7
- Ryan JM, Fleggson M, Beavis J, Macnab C. Fast-track surgical referral in a population displaced by war and conflict. *J R Soc Med* 2003;96:56-9

11   Approaches to conflict resolution

Ewan W Anderson

The potential for conflict is almost limitless, and it is impossible to prepare a recipe for resolution that will fit every occasion. Conflict may be on any scale from an individual to entire states; and no one can be an expert on all forms of conflict resolution. The most that can be asked is that aid workers have an awareness of the issues and can, if required, make some positive contribution to resolution.

Local level conflict

Conflict may start in the mind of one person and spill over to affect the local community. By focusing on that person, an aid worker may be able to defuse the conflict. On this scale, the skills required are those associated with guidance and counselling. Both sides in any negotiation need to have
- A demonstrable understanding of the issue
- A degree of empathy
- A feeling of immediacy, that something must be done
- Shared confidence that it is possible to reach a solution.

Thus the aid worker must have a thorough knowledge of the problem, a positive relationship with the person involved, and confidence that a solution can be found. Such confidence is only likely to come from prior thought and planning. The aid worker should then be able to rely on counselling skills during subsequent discussions.

However, conflicts are more likely to concern groups than clearly identifiable individuals (though individuals are normally members of a group, so personal conflict can be seen as the simplest stage of group conflict). Group conflict can occur as intra-group conflict (when members of a group conflict with one another) or inter-group conflict (when there is a conflict between separate groups). Definitions depend on the viewpoint of the observer; for an aid worker, the main distinction must be practical and concern effectiveness. Can the situation be improved or resolved by work with one or a small number of selected individuals or does it require group work?

Is conflict productive or destructive?

Conflict can be productive in that, as a result of listening to other perspectives, a solution may be found through natural negotiation or collaboration. Conflict is destructive when issues are left unresolved or there is coercion and dominance by one group over others. Destructive conflict requires more positive input from aid workers for it to be resolved.

The key factors that allow aid workers to assess the situation are assertiveness and cooperation. To what degree does each group display each of these features?

Timing can be crucial. Conflict tends to develop through stages, from an awareness that differences exist to a hardening of attitudes and, possibly, open hostility. Cooperation is more easily achieved in the initial stages of conflict, and so an earlier intervention is likely to be simpler and more effective.

Once the setting and nature of the conflict have been established, the focus must be on the perceived cause. The causes of conflict may be subsumed under three headings:
- The issues central to the conflict—political, military, economic, social, legal, technological, cultural, and physical

War damaged Afghan market

Basic principles of conflict resolution

- Paying attention—The person and the problem must receive total attention
- Listening—This requires total focus and concentration
- Reassurance—Show that the argument is being understood and include the use of open questions

---

Stages in conflict resolution

- Background—The history and all issues relevant to the problem must be collected
- Planning—Develop the framework of a plan that is positive, achievable, and relevant
- First meeting—Show empathy and knowledge of the issue; introduce for discussion the approach that might be adopted
- Subsequent meetings—Emphasise any successes achieved during discussion and, as a result, plan for future meetings
- Final meeting—Production of agreed report, with assurance of continuing support

---

Azeri women's group meeting

- The people, individually or in groups, involved in the conflict
- The overall organisation and structure within which the conflict takes place.

Key to understanding the issues is access to reliable, accurate, and complete data. An aid worker trying to resolve a conflict must have, as far as possible, full knowledge of all the relevant factors and how they interact. In conflicts, however, misinformation and disinformation all too often prevail.

The most important causes of conflict probably relate to the characteristics of the groups involved, their interests, values, and aims. If these are completely opposed, there is little room for manoeuvre. However, a seemingly fixed position may be rooted in misperception. Values may differ substantively, but they may merely seem to do so as a result of different criteria used to evaluate them. Apparently incompatible interests may be reconciled in the way an outcome is engineered. Conflict resolution means eliminating the conflict to the satisfaction of all the parties involved.

Ideally, management will result in a situation where negotiation leads directly to an agreed solution. The advantage of this method is that resolution is achieved by the opposing groups and the final solution is owned jointly.

Destructive conflict must be confronted so that the tension is reduced to an acceptable level. With detailed background knowledge of the groups involved, the issues, and the causes of the conflict, an aid worker is in a good position to intervene and ensure that a win or lose situation can be avoided

National level conflict

At this level, an aid worker will not play a central part in resolution unless specially trained. The role is likely to be one of facilitator, collector of evidence, purveyor of viewpoints, and provider of guidance and support for the experts involved. Depending on the situation, the work might be for one side in the conflict only or for all sides. Therefore, the prerequisite is knowledge of how the system might work and what might be required to ensure an equitable outcome.

At the national level, conflict intensity is likely to be greater than can normally be generated by local level conflicts, and on the global scale results are likely to be considerably more important. Several classifications for such conflict exist.

Once national interests seem to be at stake, a country's military is likely to be involved. Humanitarian aid workers are often ambivalent about the participation of the military. They may therefore operate with the military in the interests of conflict resolution but may also be in a position to act as spokespeople for the interests, rights, and values of the local population. This dual role allows a clear separation in function from that of the military.

In most cases, the basic settlement procedure is negotiation. This is effected by direct dialogue (particularly face to face), between the parties. Negotiations may lead to an agreement or may act as an initial stage, after which a joint commission is set up to agree settlement or there is some form of adjudication. Efforts may be made to insulate the adjudication process from the negotiations so that what is said in negotiations does not prejudice the final settlement. Ground rules for the negotiation may be agreed by the parties, including a time limit, after which the case is abandoned or some other avenue is pursued. The parties retain full control of proceedings throughout negotiations and are not legally bound by the outcome.

If negotiation is judged inappropriate or proves ineffective then, with the consent of all parties, a third party is invited to intervene. Depending on the degree of the intervention, it can be termed good offices, mediation, or conciliation.

Management strategies for conflict resolution

- Ensure that each side of the conflict is treated equally in all respects
- Check that each side has made its case and understood the case of the opposition
- Encourage negotiation, including compromise
- Control the discussion, focusing on the case and eliminating threats
- Impose intermissions or postponements when appropriate
- Decide if the meeting should be abandoned
- Defuse stressful situations
- Encourage the development of empathy
- Summarise key arguments, if necessary reducing some to the absurd
- Encourage sharing
- Use and encourage humour
- Judge when the situation is appropriate for more formal resolution

Example of conflict resolution: Uganda

One conflict concerned whether government funding should be spent on the sinking of a new well or the enhancement of all the main spring sources. The case was presented to all the involved village councils and then to the local regional council. As a result, an agreement was reached on enhancement

Classifications of national conflict

- High intensity warfare
- Low intensity warfare
- Covert military action
- Political action such as terrorist action
- Diplomatic action such as closure of boundaries
- Economic actions such as boycotts and sanctions
- Verbal expressions

Ethnic cleansing in Bosnia

Definitions in conflict resolution

- *Good offices*—A third party merely acts as a communications link between the two opposing sides and represents an enhancement of communications.
- *Mediation*—A third party not only acts as a communications link but is an active participant in the negotiations and is encouraged to contribute to them
- *Conciliation*—This is normally implemented by a commission rather than an individual. The commission requires terms of reference agreed by all parties, and the third party thereby has a legal basis for operation

Examples of national level settlements in which the author has been involved include the production of scientific background material for the boundary cases of Saudi Arabia, all of which ended by negotiation. Cartographic and scientific research was completed for the maritime and land boundaries of Libya, all cases resulting in decision by judicial settlement. In addition, the direction of a range of surveys and data collection exercises enabled two administrative groups in northern Iraq to appreciate the real situation within their jointly run territory and to work more closely together.

Mid-level conflict

For mid-level disputes such as those between tribes or regional governments, there are opportunities for aid workers to operate in both roles. The main causes of conflict at this level are

- Data—lack of information, misinformation, disinformation, and differing interpretations or perceptions
- Interests—these may refer to the procedure for settlement or the needs of the opposing groups
- Values—these include different aims, lifestyles, ideologies, and religious beliefs and have a major influence on the evaluation of any settlement.

At this level of resolution, less institutionalised, more imaginative procedures can be envisaged. The US Army Corps of Engineers has developed a series of alternative dispute resolution procedures. These include development of role play, important at the local level of settlement, into a rather more formal mini-trial. The disputants would go through the procedures of a trial, but the decision would not be binding. A further development of this is non-binding arbitration.

At the less formal end of proceedings, aid workers can be active participants, whether as managers or mediators. With increased formality, the role becomes more one of offering support and providing evidence. For all settlement procedures, data about the issue, the disputants, and the causes of the conflict are vital. Through practical involvement with the people in dispute, aid workers are in a particularly advantageous position to help facilitate conflict resolution, whichever procedure is selected.

Competing interests: None declared.

Landmine clearance centre. Removal of unexploded mines and ordnance is an essential part of conflict resolution

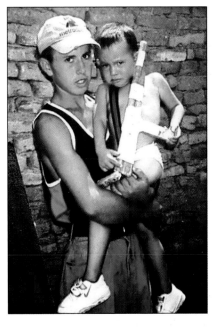

Experiencing conflict can have a profound impact on children, potentially leading to further conflict by new generations

Further reading

- Merrills JG. *International dispute settlement*. 2nd ed. Cambridge: Cambridge University Press, 1993
- Horwath J, Morrison T. *Effective staff training in social care*. London: Routledge, 1999
- Doel M, Sawdon C. *The essential groupworker*. London: Jessica Kingsley, 1999

12 Weapons of mass destruction—threats and responses

Christine Gosden, Derek Gardener

Weapons of mass destruction (WMD) include chemical, biological, and radiological agents with the potential to cause death at low doses and with serious long term health effects in survivors. This article provides general information relevant to all situations, from terrorist attacks in developed countries to conflict zones in Third World countries. WMD agents can be used to terrorise or subjugate populations and wreak economic damage. Many agents are cheap to produce and can be deployed in different ways. As well as overt use, such as in bombs or by aerial spraying, they can be used covertly such as in packages sent in the post, via animal vectors, or by poisoning of water and food supplies.

Casualties from the attack on Halabja in northern Iraq by the former Iraqi government with multiple WMD agents, including nerve and mustard agents

Threats from WMD

The classic scenario of WMD use against civilians (the basis of many current exercises) is the release of the nerve agent sarin in the Tokyo subway. In this attack the actions of first responders and medical staff helped keep the final fatalities down to 12. Because they lacked protective clothing, however, many of these people absorbed sarin from victims' clothing and developed serious long term neurological complications. Other agents—such as mustard agent, VX, anthrax, and radiation—are more persistent and thus pose greater risks: doses to victims would be higher, attending staff would face protracted periods in protective clothing, and the threat would remain until full decontamination was achieved.

The diversity and gravity of threats are exemplified by the recent anthrax attack on the US Congress through the postal system. It claimed few victims, thanks to rapid intervention by bioweapons specialists, but it paralysed the postal system and cost over $6bn to clean up.

For the past seven years we have collaborated in a programme to treat and study the immediate and long term effects of WMD on the people of Halabja in northern Iraq. Our experiences have led us to draw up information about the risks from WMD agents, decontamination, immediate and long term effects, and responses to help victims and protect responders.

Diversity of WMD agents

The range of potential WMD agents and delivery mechanisms is extensive. For chemical weapons, as well as highly toxic and persistent new agents such as VX, older agents, such as mustard gas, remain highly dangerous and relatively easy to obtain. For biological agents, the key element is rapid identification so that countermeasures can be deployed before the agent is widely disseminated. Biological toxins resemble chemical agents rather than infectious organisms: they can pose major threats, but usually only over localised areas or to poison food or water. Radiological weapons include weaponised radioactive waste and dirty bombs as well as nuclear weapons.

Chemical weapons: agents and effects
Chemical agents include vesicants (blister or mustard agents), nerve agents (sarin, soman, tabun, and VX), and blood agents (cyanide).

Threats from weapons of mass destruction

- Threats overt or covert
- Delivery systems include bombs, shells, spraying, mines, hand grenades, animal vectors (such as fleas)
- Strategic and economic targets—Administrative and key centres, animals, crops, food
- More than one agent may be used in an attack

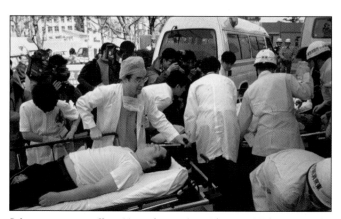

Subway passengers affected by sarin gas planted in central Tokyo attended by unprotected first responders and medical staff

In the attack on Halabja 5000 civilians died immediately. The entire town of 80 000 was overcome, and there was no one to respond or provide medical support. The agents used included powerful and persistent carcinogens, resulting in many survivors with major long term illness

The former government of Iraq often used mustard and nerve agents in the same attack and weaponised chemical agents mixed with biological agents such as anthrax and aflatoxin. Use of more than one agent can lead to difficulties in detecting all the agents involved, increase mortality, complicate symptoms, and make decontamination more difficult

Mustard agent causes immediate severe damage to the respiratory tract, skin, and eyes, but skin blisters and corneal effects are not usually apparent for minutes to hours, though the characteristic garlic odour and burning sensation in throat and eyes may provide earlier warning. The carcinogenic effects of mustard agent begin within 2-4 minutes, and there are no antidotes. Long term effects include cancers; damage to respiratory, immune, and reproductive systems; and blindness. Victims need rapid decontamination to minimise effects.

Nerve agents may be colourless and odourless and give little warning of their presence, but minute amounts can kill rapidly. Their immediate effects can be recognised with the acronym DUMBELS (diarrhoea; urination; miosis; bradycardia, bronchorrhoea, and bronchospasm; emesis; lacrimation; and salivation and sweating). Victims—especially those without protective clothing, gas masks, or antidotes—rapidly become unconscious, have breathing difficulties, and may die. Sarin, tabun, and soman are relatively non-persistent but tend to "off gas" as they evaporate, which can present a vapour hazard for first responders. VX persists for several days and is over 150 times more toxic than sarin and tabun and is therefore very dangerous. Warning signs may include symptoms or death in animals, birds, and insects. Nerve agents can have various long term effects from cardiac arrhythmias to major neuropathies.

Cyanide is extremely light and disperses rapidly in the open air but is dangerous at high concentrations in enclosed spaces.

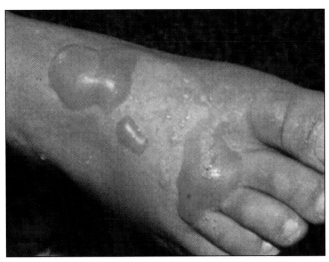

Characteristic blistering of skin from exposure to mustard agent. The blisters resolve, but 30% of mustard agent victims have severe, irreversible damage to the skin, eyes, and lungs. Even those lacking these symptoms are at risk of serious future problems. Medical authorities should be concerned about all victims' future health and wellbeing

Chemical WMD agents and their properties

Agent	Physical characteristics	Lethal dose (LD_{50})	Time to onset of symptoms	Principal effects
Vesicants				
Mustard agents	Colourless to brown oily liquid; garlic or mustard odour	7 g/person	15 minutes to 4 hours	Blisters, eye irritation, tearing, cough, dyspnoea, pulmonary oedema, nausea, vomiting, diarrhoea, anxiety
Nerve agents				
Tabun	Colourless liquid; slight fruity odour	1 g/person		Increased salivation and bronchial secretions, cough, dyspnoea
Sarin	Colourless liquid; faintly sweet odour	1.7 g/person	Seconds to minutes	Miosis, tearing, nausea, vomiting, abdominal cramp, diarrhoea, involuntary defecation and micturition
Soman	Colourless liquid; camphor odour	0.35 g/person		Apprehension, headache, confusion, ataxia, weakness, coma, convulsions, paralysis
VX	Colourless or amber oily liquid; odourless	0.01 g/person		
Blood agent				
Hydrogen cyanide	Colourless or grey crystalline solid; sharp, irritating floral odour	7 g/person	Immediate	Dyspnoea, eye irritation, nausea, vomiting, depression, headache, ataxia, convulsions, coma

Responses to chemical WMD

An effective response to chemical WMD requires chemical detection or monitoring systems, antidotes where appropriate, rapid decontamination, and ensuring that exposed populations do not consume contaminated food and water or remain in contaminated environments. The sarin attack in Tokyo showed the vulnerability of civilian populations, first responders, and medical teams. Victims were overcome by a colourless, odourless, volatile agent; delays in identifying the responsible agent allowed contamination to extend to receiving hospitals, where staff failed to put on protective clothing and gas masks.

Antidotes for nerve agents include atropine, which works by blocking acetylcholine at the postsynaptic receptor sites, thus counteracting muscarinic effects. Because atropine does not affect nicotinic synapses, oximes such as pralidoxime are also given. Oximes bind with acetylcholinesterase and hydrolyse the nerve agent, but are effective only if given soon after exposure, otherwise nerve agent binding becomes irreversible. Because nerve agents act rapidly, responders must put on gas masks and protective clothing immediately to avoid becoming casualties themselves.

Responses to food contaminated with chemical agents (mustard or nerve agents)

High fat foods (butter, fats, eggs, cheese, meat)
- Condemn if exposed to agents in liquid or vapour form

Low fat foods
High moisture (fruit, vegetables, sugar, salt)
Low moisture (cereal, tea, coffee, flour, bread, rice)
- Condemn if exposed to agents in liquid form
- If exposed to agents in vapour form:
  Expose dry food to air for 48 hours
  Wash other foods in 2% sodium bicarbonate
  Peel where applicable
  Cook by boiling

It is important not to delay decontamination. In the absence of specialised decontamination, household bleach (sodium hypochlorite) should be used. This is effective against nerve and mustard agents and many bioweapons, but it requires clear instructions about the correct dilution (1 in 10, such as 1 litre of bleach in 9 litres water) and of special precautions such as avoiding the eyes. Although direct contact with such a bleach solution would normally be considered unwise, rapid decontamination may save lives, especially for fast acting, highly toxic agents such as VX. In Halabja, Iraq, thousands died immediately and many survivors have severe long term problems because no decontamination was carried out on victims, the environment, or the unexploded bombs that harboured large amounts of native nerve and mustard agents.

Bioweapons: bacteria, viruses, and toxins

Many potential biological agents exist, but we will consider only high risk (category A) agents. These pose the greatest threat to public health, may spread across large areas, carry a high risk of death, and are readily transmissible from person to person or are easily disseminated. The dangers are greatest when no vaccines or effective treatments are available.

Protection, prophylaxis, and treatment

Bioweapons can be countered by recognition of risks, accurate diagnosis, and rapid treatment. For most agents, specialised testing is necessary by public health specialists or laboratories. For bacterial agents, vaccination and treatment with antibiotics or antitoxins must be started early to prevent disease progression and death. For viral diseases, vaccination is the principal form of prophylaxis: the use of antiviral drugs might be useful, but effectiveness and safety have yet to be established.

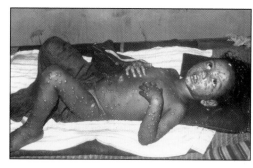

Smallpox is very contagious, and lack of natural resistance or vaccine means it would be highly lethal

Biological agents of mass destruction

Agents with direct person to person transmission
- Include bacterial and viral diseases
- Obviate the need for specialised weapons delivery systems
- Many contacts may be infected and the disease widely disseminated before the outbreak is recognised

Agents with no or rare person to person transmission
- Include bacterial agents and biological toxins
- Easily disseminated and can pose major threats, such as the risks to staff and the cost of decontaminating US government buildings after anthrax was released via the postal system
- Toxins can be derived from diverse organisms and have a wide spectrum of effects varying from immediate lethality (botulinum toxin, ricin) to long term carcinogenicity (aflatoxin and other mycotoxins)

Biological WMD agents (class A) and their properties

Agent	Transmission mode	Incubation and lethality	Symptoms	Prophylaxis and treatment
Direct person to person transmission				
Bacterial				
Plague (pneumonic or bubonic)	Aerosol droplets or flea vectors	1-6 days. High lethality unless treated	Fever, weakness, cough, respiratory failure, pneumonia	Antibiotics (streptomycin, gentamicin, tetracyclines)
Cholera	Contaminated food or water	Hours. 20-25% lethality if untreated	Watery diarrhoea, vomiting, leg cramps. Death can be in hours	Vaccines (not in US). Prompt rehydration. Antibiotics
Typhoid	Contaminated food or water	3 days to 8 weeks. Moderate lethality	Fever, weakness, pain, headache	Vaccine. Antibiotics (but resistance emerging)
Viral				
Smallpox	Direct contact, body fluids	7-17 days. High lethality	High fever, rash, severe aches, headache, abdominal pain	Vaccine
Viral haemorrhagic fevers (Ebola, Lassa, Marburg)	Nosocomial (possible animal reservoir)	2-21 days. High lethality	High fever, severe prostration, haemorrhage, petechiae, oedema, myalgia, headache	Supportive treatment (need stringent infection control, VHF barrier precautions)
No or rare person to person transmission				
Bacterial				
Anthrax	Spores, aerosol, food	1-5 days. High lethality unless treated	Fever, malaise, cough, shock. Death can be within 36 hours	Vaccine. Antibiotics (ciprofloxacin, doxycycline)
Tularaemia	Aerosols, tick or insect bites, contaminated food or water	3-14 days. Moderate lethality if untreated	Sudden onset acute febrile illness, cough, weakness	Live attenuated vaccine. Antibiotics (gentamicin, streptomycin). Protect against biting arthropods
Biological toxins				
Aflatoxin	Aerosol, contaminated food or water	Variable time. Lethality depends on dose and route of exposure	Fever, wheezing, cough. Liver damage, stillbirths, birth defects, cancer	Testing, removal of contaminated food
Botulinum toxin	Aerosol, contaminated food or water	6 hours to 14 days. High lethality	Blurred vision, difficulty swallowing, muscle weakness, paralysis of respiratory muscles	Antitoxin effective if given early. Supportive care, ventilation
Staphylococcus enterotoxin B	Aerosol, contaminated food or water	1-6 hours. Lethality <1%	Vomiting, nausea, diarrhoea, chest pain, headache, myalgia	No antidotes, vaccine, or antitoxins. Supportive care, ventilation
Ricin	Aerosol, contaminated food or water	Hours to days. High lethality	Fever, dyspnoea, nausea, pulmonary oedema	No vaccine or antitoxins. Supportive care, ventilation for severe cases

Radiological weapons

Nuclear devices are unmistakable because of the thermal blast, but radiological dispersal devices such as dirty bombs (conventional explosives laced with radioactive isotopes in the form of pellets or powder) may not be immediately recognised if monitoring with a Geiger counter is not done. Monitoring (including identifying contaminated food, water, and milk) is crucial in any radiological incident, as are decontamination and providing iodine tablets if radioiodine is released.

Management of mass casualties

Given the wide array of WMD and delivery mechanisms, preparedness for all possible events is extremely challenging. The basis of an effective response involves

- Stay upwind and uphill
- Monitor to identify agents (more than one may be used)
- Decontaminate or isolate people affected
- Give antidotes as appropriate for nerve agents
- Provide treatment for bioweapons (antibiotics, vaccination)
- Provide respiratory support if necessary (respiratory paralysis is a common primary event that is often temporary), but remember that victims may pose a risk to responders who lack adequate protection
- Good communication and coordination of information from pharmacies, laboratories, first responders, emergency medicine, and medical and public health staff
- Deal swiftly with any contaminated food, water, and environment to prevent casualties extending beyond those directly affected (the main cancers among survivors of the atomic bombs dropped on Japan were of the gut because of ingestion of contaminated food and water)
- Preparedness measures include supplies of bottled water and safe food stored in non-permeable containers.

Long term effects of WMD

The long term health effects of WMD depend on the agent used, dose, route of exposure, and victims' genetic susceptibility. The Japanese atomic bombs resulted in cancers, infertility, and adverse pregnancy outcomes. Mustard agent can cause cancers of the head, neck, and respiratory tract, haematological malignancies, immune system dysfunction, infertility, and birth defects in offspring. Long term effects of nerve agents include neurological and psychiatric problems and cardiac arrhythmias.

Fetuses are especially vulnerable because, unlike children and adults, they lack most of the protective mechanisms for metabolising or protecting against WMD agents (thus, rates of leukaemia among the survivors of the Hiroshima bomb were far greater for those exposed in utero than for other age groups).

There has been little study or acknowledgment of the long term risks of WMD, because people have concentrated almost exclusively on short term problems. Long term risks may be severe and life threatening, but the lack of recognition of the sequelae means survivors receive no help.

Reducing these effects depends on deploying effective detection systems to alert to WMD risks, establishing systems for rapid responses with facilities for decontamination and treatment of casualties, providing information to the affected population, and providing uncontaminated food, water, and environment after an attack.

Competing interests: None declared.

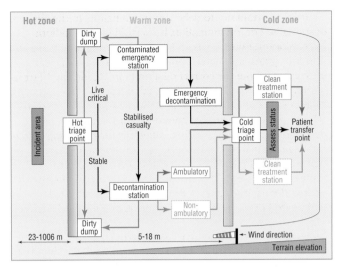

Procedure for dealing with casualties from a WMD incident

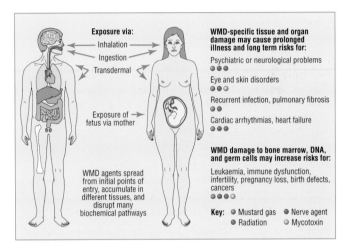

Long term effects of WMD. These may be serious, depending on the agent, route of exposure, dose, and individual susceptibility. Prompt actions, such as decontamination, help to mitigate against long term health problems

Further reading

- Ellison, DH. *Handbook of chemical and biological warfare agents.* Boca Raton, FL: CRC Press, 2000
- Dwyer A, Eldridge J, Kernan M. *Jane's chem-bio handbook international.* 2nd ed. Coulsdon: Jane's Information Group, 2003
- National Guideline Clearinghouse. Guidelines on bioterrorism. www.guideline.gov/resources/bioterrorism.aspx
- Health Protection Agency. www.hpa.org.uk
- CDC Centers for Disease Control and Prevention. Emergency preparedness and response. www.bt.cdc.gov
- World Health Organization. *Public health response to biological and chemical weapons: WHO guidance.* Geneva: WHO, 2004. (www.who.int/csr/delibepidemics/biochemguide/en/)

The picture of the Halabja massacre is reproduced with permission of CNN/Getty. The picture of the Tokyo subway attack is reproduced with permission of Chikumo Chiaki/AP/Empics. The picture of mustard gas blisters is supplied by Defence Science and Technology Laboratory, Porton Down, Salisbury. The picture of smallpox is supplied by the CDC Public Health Image Library.

Index

Index